THE GOOD, THE BAD, AND THE GRACE OF GOD

What Honesty and Pain Taught Us About
Faith, Family, and Forgiveness

JEP ROBERTSON AND JESSICA ROBERTSON

with Susy Flory

W Publishing Group

An Imprint of Thomas Nelson

Published in Nashville, Tennessee, by W Publishing Group, an imprint of Thomas Nelson.

Thomas Nelson titles may be purchased in bulk for educational, business, fund-raising, or sales promotional use. For information, please e-mail SpecialMarkets@ ThomasNelson.com.

Scripture quotations marked NASB are taken from the New American Standard Bible®, © 1960, 1962, 1963, 1968, 1971, 1972, 1973, 1975, 1977, 1995 by The Lockman Foundation. Used by permission. www.Lockman.org.

Scripture quotations marked NLT are taken from the Holy Bible, New Living Translation. © 1996, 2004, 2007 by Tyndale House Foundation. Used by permission of Tyndale House Publishers Inc., Carol Stream, IL 60188. All rights reserved.

Scripture quotations marked NIV are taken from the Holy Bible, New International Version®, NIV®. © 1973, 1978, 1984, 2011 by Biblica, Inc.™ Used by permission of Zondervan. All rights reserved worldwide.

Scripture quotations marked ESV are taken from the ESV® Bible (The Holy Bible, English Standard Version®), © 2001 by Crossway, a publishing ministry of Good News Publishers. Used by permission. All rights reserved.

Library of Congress Control Number: 2015932949

ISBN 978-0-7180-3148-0

Printed in the United States of America

15 16 17 18 19 RRD 6 5 4 3 2 1

We would like to dedicate our book to our children: Lily, Merritt, Priscilla, and River. We are so grateful that God blessed us with four miracles. Seeing life come into this world has been life changing.

We hope that our life journey can better equip you for the world and that you can learn from our struggles and mistakes. More importantly, we hope you know God Almighty is there with you always; He loves you, and nothing you do will ever change that.

Contents

CONTENTS

Acknowledgments

THANK YOU, JESUS, FOR WHAT YOU'VE DONE, ARE DOING, AND WILL continue to do for a good ole boy from North Louisiana. Thank you, God, for the best parents a man could ever hope for.

My incredible brothers, thanks for always having my back and showing me how men of God are supposed to live. My terrific sisters-in-law, thanks for putting up with my bros and being good friends and mentors for Jess.

My "blood brothers"—Fishbone, Nicky Tightpants, McG, G.G., ZDash, Maxi—and all the countless friends who've been there through the good, the bad, and the grace of God.

—Jep

THANK YOU, GOD, FOR THE DEATH, BURIAL, AND RESURRECTION OF Jesus Christ. Without it, I would have no hope.

Thanks, Mom and Dad, for all you've done for me. Thanks, Stacy, for being such a wonderful sister; you and Andy have always been there for me.

To my sistas—Emily, Tara, Ashleigh, Jil, Erica—and all my gals: you are all amazing women of God and bless my life. Thanks for being such great friends and being there for me through the best and toughest of times.

To Korie, Missy, and Lisa: you are three of the most amazing women, and I'm honored to call you sisters and friends. Kay, you will never know the impact you have made in my life. You and Phil have shown Jep and me how to love each other for better or for worse and how to forgive and move forward. To my bros-in-law: you seriously are the best brothers a girl could ever ask for. Thanks for the commitment you all made to stay close to your family. It's a legacy of faith and family that will be passed on for generations to come.

—Jessica

WE ALSO WANT TO SAY THANKS TO MEL, MARGARET, AND MATT FOR believing in our story. To Jessie, Deana, and all the WME agents: thanks for all your hard work. Y'all are the best!

—Jep and Jessica

Love Letters

LOVE LETTERS HAVE ALWAYS BEEN A BIG PART OF OUR LIVES.

We've written love letters to each other.

Miss Kay wrote some very special letters to Jep (her favorite) at a crucial time in his life.

Jessica has been writing letters—some long, some short—to our kids, Lily, Merritt, Priscilla, and River. She pours out whatever is on her mind or in her heart at that moment for them to read when they grow up.

Now our girls have taken up writing love letters, mostly to us and to their mamaws. Perhaps someday they'll be writing to their husbands too.

But the most precious letter of all is one that we treasure most— God's love letter to us. Without it, we'd still be lost. Studying God's words together was part of what kept us together when everything else was tearing us apart. God is the glue that holds our marriage together.

We are like the rest of the Robertson family. We care much more about love than money or fame or expensive toys. We care about our children and family and friends and being together. We want more than anything else to be rich in love.

This is the story of how we met and how our love started when we had both stumbled and struggled to find our way in life and were losing hope. It's also the story of how forgiveness can break down the barriers that stand in your way, put you on the path of grace, and give you a fresh new start.

This is our story, both the good and the bad.

This is our love letter to you.

—Jep and Jessica

ONE

Knight in Shining Camo

Jep and Jess

Life is so full of unpredictable beauty and strange surprises.

—Mark Oliver Everett, *Things the Grandchildren Should Know*

ONCE UPON A TIME A GIRL FROM TOWN MET A BOY FROM THE WOODS.

Even back then, it was all about the hair. I was at Connie Sue's in West Monroe to get my long hair colored, cut, and blown out. When he opened the door and walked in, I looked up, and there he was.

Jep.

I'm the fourth son of a fourth son. My name is Jules Jeptha Robertson, and I have three older brothers, Alan, Jase, and Willie. You might have heard of them.

Most people call me Jep, but my first name is Jules. Mom and

1

Dad named me after the hero in the Yul Brynner movie *Invitation to a Gunfighter*. My middle name is Jeptha, after a great-grandfather who died in a shootout over a land dispute. There's also a Jephthah in the Bible, spelled with two extra *h*'s. He was a judge and led the people of Israel into battle against a group of people called the Ammonites. The Israelites won.

Maybe it's not a coincidence that I've always been interested in heroes, starting with my dad, Phil Robertson, and my mom, Miss Kay. My other heroes are my pa and my granny, who taught me how to play cards and dominoes and everything about fishing (which was a lot), and my three older brothers, who teased me, beat me up, and sometimes let me follow them around. Not much has changed in that department.

I've always loved movies, and when I was about seven or eight years old, I watched *Rocky*, Sylvester Stallone's movie about an underdog boxer who used his fists, along with sheer will, determination, and the ability to endure pain, to make a way for himself. He fought hard but played fair and had a soft spot for his friends. I fell in love with Rocky. He was my hero, and I became obsessed.

When I decide to do something, I'm all in; so I found a pair of red shorts that looked like Rocky's boxing trunks and a navy blue bathrobe with two white stripes on the sleeve and no belt. I took off my shirt and ran around bare-chested in my robe and shorts. Most kids I knew went through a superhero phase, but they picked DC Comics guys, like Batman or Superman. Not me. I was Rocky Balboa, the Italian Stallion, and proud of it. Mom let me run around like that for a couple of years, even when we went in to town.

Rocky had a girlfriend, Adrian, who was always there, always by his side. When he was beaten and blinded in a bad fight, he called out for her before anybody else. "Yo, Adrian!" he shouted in his Philly-Italian accent. He needed her.

Eventually, I grew up, and the red shorts and blue bathrobe didn't fit anymore, but I always remembered Rocky's kindness and his courage. And that every Rocky needs an Adrian.

––––––––––

While Jep was running around in the woods, down by the river, I could be found climbing a tree, going hunting with my dad, or picking vegetables in the garden with my mamaw Nellie and papaw Ted. I come from a family of hunters and fishermen; even my grandmother Lola hunted. I loved getting up early and drinking coffee with Dad before we hit the road to hunting camp, and I became a pretty good shot.

I was not an indoor kind of little girl. I had loads of energy, big dreams, and a happy heart. Today they'd probably say I had ADD/ADHD, but that's just me—I give my all to everything I do, and I've always been that way. That's why I love being outdoors. There was always so much to do, and I wanted to do it all. I've never liked to sit still—I love to keep myself busy.

I was also a born people-pleaser, and I spent my childhood trying to make my parents happy. Once, when I was about ten years old, I hadn't missed a day of school all year, and I was excited about earning a perfect attendance award again, just like I had the year before. I was looking forward to how proud my parents and my teacher would be.

But one morning a freak accident occurred, putting my award in jeopardy. I was in the bathroom, getting ready for school, when Mom called my name. I turned my head to answer, my neck caught, and all of a sudden I felt a strong jolt of searing pain. *What is wrong with my neck?* I thought in agony.

There was no way in the world I was going to miss getting my award or let my parents and teacher down, so I tried to ignore the excruciating crick in my neck. Instead, I decided to try to turn my whole body, gritting my teeth and bearing the pain; but I just couldn't do it. I broke the news to my mom. She took one look at me and quickly decided we'd have to go see the doctor.

I burst out crying. "I really need to get that perfect attendance award," I sobbed.

"Jessica, your teacher will understand," Mom reassured me. "She won't be disappointed in you, and you will survive."

I didn't get the perfect attendance award that year. But I did earn a surprise award, named the Betty Crocker Award. The principal created it especially for me because I'd almost burned down my house earlier that year. One day, right before she left for work, Mom had mixed up a batch of biscuits for my breakfast and popped them in the oven.

"Jessica, watch those biscuits and take them out of the oven when they're done," she called out as she left the house for her teaching job at a little country school on the outskirts of West Monroe.

"Okay, Mom," I called back.

But soon after that, the school bus arrived. I ran outside, completely forgetting the biscuits. About an hour into the school day, my stomach started to growl, and I thought, *Hmm, that's weird. I know I had biscuits for breakfast. Wait! No, I didn't. I forgot to get them out of the oven!*

I could practically smell them burning, and I ran up to the front in a panic and told my teacher, who sent me to the office to tell the principal what had happened. Mr. Smith seemed a little worried and decided to drive me home to check on the house. Just as we turned onto my street, we saw a big red fire truck pulling up to the front of our house. Then I heard the smoke alarms going off. I was embarrassed, but I still had to go into the house with Mr. Smith and the firefighters, who wanted to make sure there wasn't a real fire. The biscuits had been transformed into charred little black lumps, earning me the one and only Betty Crocker Award ever given out at my school. It wasn't the perfect attendance award, but at least I'd won *some* kind of award.

I was a busy child and never grew out of it, so I was moving fast as usual when I passed Jep that day on my way out of Connie Sue's salon. But not too fast to notice his thick dark hair, cut just above his ears and brushed back, with sexy Elvis chops on the sides. He had deep green eyes, a strong jaw, and a small, dark soul patch under his bottom lip that stood out against his tanned skin.

Our eyes locked, and I was mesmerized. His steps slowed, and he tilted his head down a little, smiled a sweet smile, and said, "Hey."

Did I mention the dimples? He had the cutest dimples I'd ever seen. My heart seriously skipped a beat, although I tried not to let it show. (I always tell him he had me at "hey," and that's no joke.)

"Hey," I said back.

I wish I could tell you I said something original and witty, but that's all I could come up with. A nod and a "hey." Then he was gone.

Who is he?

Jep was twenty-two, I was twenty, and somehow we'd grown up in the same town and never met each other. And even though we were young, we both already had complicated lives. We had experienced pain, guilt, betrayal, and brokenness.

But in that moment, none of it mattered. Not one bit.

As I headed to the chair for a haircut, I wondered who she was. Long, silky blonde hair, parted on the side. Fair skin. Blue eyes with thick lashes. And a big, friendly smile. I thought I might have seen her once at a party, but I hadn't talked to her, and I wasn't sure.

"Who was that?" I asked Connie Sue as I sat down.

"Her name's Jessica," said Connie Sue. "She's been through a lot lately, but she's a sweet girl."

As I drove home, I kept replaying that moment over and over when our eyes met. I saw her face, her beautiful smile, and heard her warm voice again.

I wish I'd said something more.

When I got home, I walked in the front door of my rental house with Jessica still on my mind. My roommate, Trey, was sitting on the couch, holding a video game controller and staring at the TV.

"Hey," I said again, this time with confidence.

He looked up, a little irritated I was interrupting his game.

"I just met the girl I'm going to marry."

TWO

Granny's Boy

Jep

There's no place like home . . . except Granny's.

—Anonymous

LIFE STARTED OFF GOOD FOR ME. FIVE YEARS HAD PASSED SINCE DAD'S dramatic conversion from hard-drinking river rat to faithful husband and father, entrepreneur, and follower of Christ. Now he was sober and in a good place. After I arrived, Mom went right back to being busy, working long hours trying to help Dad get Duck Commander, his new business making duck calls, off the ground and to make enough money to support our family of six.

I had three older brothers, but Alan, who was already fifteen when I was born, moved out two years later and wasn't around much. Jase and Willie were nine and seven years old, so by the time I was old enough to play, they were busy doing older-kid stuff. I was the baby of the family and the apple of my mom's eye. I'm her favorite, remember? But I had a granny who loved me an awful lot too.

Granny and Pa had moved to West Monroe when my parents bought a piece of property on the Ouachita River, right where Cypress Creek splits off to flow into a peaceful patch of water called Thompson's Bayou, just beyond the front yard of our little two-bedroom house. Dad didn't have the money for a down payment, so Granny and Pa helped. While I was growing up, they lived just down the driveway from us in an old green house with a loud, creaky screen door.

I spent just about every day at Granny's. Granny and I were very close. Many a night my mom worked late, and I fell asleep at Granny's until Mom came to pick me up and carry me home and put me to bed. Granny was my dad's mother, and her real name was Merritt Thurman Hale Robertson. She was strong and clever, one of the thousands of Rosie the Riveters who helped build bombs during World War II. When she was younger, she'd been diagnosed with manic depression and had to undergo electric shock treatment. By the time I came around, she was on lithium, which helped stabilize her ups and downs. She spent her days fishing, sometimes playing dominoes or gin with Pa, and always watching her soaps.

Pa's name was James Robertson, and he was a man of few words. He never got mad, and he never got glad. I do remember, when he was irritated, he'd squint his eyes at me and say *hmm* under his breath. But I don't remember him ever really getting mad at me. Pa had a lot of medical problems stemming from a serious back injury when he was a roughneck on an offshore oil rig. He'd fallen eighteen feet from a drilling rig, landed on his head, broke two vertebrae, and ruptured his stomach. It took him years to recover. He still suffered from the pain and didn't get around much. But he did like to play games, and

I remember watching him with my dad and his brothers, yelling at one another and slamming the dominoes down onto the table. I liked watching as they laughed, argued, and teased one another.

When I was old enough, Pa taught me how to play simple card games, such as Go Fish, before I graduated to playing gin. Granny and Pa also let me play three-man dominoes but complained if I was too slow trying to add up the numbers. I can still hear it. "Come on, Jeptha! Go ahead and play something—we're waiting."

Pa played hard and never let us win if he could help it; he felt playing dominoes taught us to add numbers quickly and develop a strategy. I did beat him a few times, but not often.

Although Granny played some with us, she was much more interested in getting out on the water. She taught me how to fish as soon as I could sit in a boat and hold a pole. A true river rat, she gave me a paddle, taught me how to use it, and had me serve as a human trolling motor on her boat. I'd bait her hook, then try to follow instructions: "Paddle over there. Keep the boat straight and let me catch one."

Dad went fishing, too, but he caught large, commercial quantities of fish in hoop nets to sell at the fish market. Granny, on the other hand, enjoyed sport fishing, catching just enough for a meal or two.

I still use Granny's bait secrets. One is to find an old rotted tree, dig through the decaying wood, find big white grubs, and stick them right on the hook. Another trick she taught me works best after a rain: find two sticks, cut a series of notches across each, then hold one stick upright touching the ground while you rub the other stick across the notches, creating a strong vibration. The worms think it's raining and come up to the surface to get air, where you can grab 'em up. The best but trickiest bait is wasp larvae. If you find a wasp nest and can tear it down and run away without getting stung too bad, those half-formed wasps will draw a lot of fish. This tasty protein drives the fish crazy, but you have to be fast.

"You're gonna learn all the spots out here," Granny told me, "how to catch 'em, what kind of fish are good, and what to do when your line breaks."

She was a patient fisherwoman and could look at the creek for a few minutes, analyze it, and quickly decide where to go. "We need to go up about a hundred yards. See that little cut over there? We'll catch fish right there."

The wide, deep creek and the bayou were full of fish—bass, crawfish, and down deeper were the prehistoric-looking alligator gar. During certain times of the year, the Opelousa catfish were running. The giant Opelousas were way bigger than me at that age, and I saw my dad catch a ninety-pounder.

We would catch bluegill, chinquapin, bream, catfish, and goggle-eye that we fried whole. But mainly we fished for crappie, the whitest fish. Crappie is best coated in cornmeal, salt, and pepper and fried up in a cast-iron skillet.

Then there were trash fish, little fish not worth eating. Granny would get mad when they'd tear off the bait or the line on her cane pole, causing her to lose her bobber. She showed me how to improvise with a chunk of Styrofoam, which makes a great bobber if you put a needle through it and tie a knot on one end. She also showed me how to use a sewing needle to make a fishing hook. And fishing licenses? She never bothered with that.

Granny owned the boat ramp, where we put the boat into the creek, and the neighbors liked to use it because we kept it in good shape. She charged people a dollar a launch, and they stuffed their bills into a little mailbox by the ramp. During the summers she would make fifty to one hundred dollars a day, and when I was old enough, she'd pay me a few dollars to collect the money for her.

When Granny caught fish, we'd head back to the house for bacon and eggs, fried in lots of grease; bacon and tomato sandwiches; peanut butter sandwiches; and buttermilk biscuits. Every once in a while she'd bake a sweet potato pie that I didn't have to share with anyone else.

Both Granny and Pa smoked all the time, and I think it affected Granny's taste buds because she liked to snack on some very strange things—many a time I saw her eat a whole, raw Vidalia onion, just like you'd eat an apple, and straight up drink a big glass of chunky buttermilk to go with it.

Maybe the buttermilk-onion combination was the culprit for one of her signature moves—every time she got up off the couch, she'd hold her stomach and then fart. Loud. She never laughed or cracked a smile, but it always made me laugh, and I pictured her using intestinal gas like a turbocharged engine to propel her off the couch. Maybe that combo helps you live until you're ninety-six, like Granny!

The nicest thing in Granny's house was her television set, and it was always blaring the soap operas, like *The Bold and the Beautiful* or *The Young and the Restless*, or a game show—no remote control, three channels only, and balls of tinfoil crumpled around the top of the antennae.

Granny was a huge fan of *The Price Is Right*, hosted by Bob Barker. She had an amazing memory for grocery-store prices and always nailed the answers. One day when she was in her eighties, Granny announced, "I'm going to California to be on *The Price Is Right*. I'm going to win it. No problem."

Granny talked my Uncle Harold into driving her to California, walker and all, and the family gathered around our television to watch Granny compete live on the country's largest game show. And Granny did it! First, she won a Ford Mustang automobile. Then when it came time to guess the value of the showcase, she won that too. She came home with a truckload of appliances and not one but two cars. She had to sell one car to pay the sales taxes, but she was a winner, and she'd done what she said she was going to do. For the rest of her life, Granny slept with a signed photo of Bob Barker right next to her bed.

I believe Granny raised me just as much as my mom and dad did. It was a great life for a kid. And thanks to Granny and Pa, I will always remember Wednesdays as Pa's bath day.

For some reason Pa hated taking baths. "Pa," Granny would say, "it's Wednesday. Get in here and get your bath."

"Hmm . . . well, if it's Wednesday, I'll take it."

Smart man. He knew better than to mess with Granny.

THREE

Tomboy

Jess

> Girls who play in dirt and mud grow up healthier.
>
> —Sharyn Clough, *Social Science & Medicine*

MY OLDER SISTER, STACY, WAS MORE ACADEMIC AND LOVED TO READ, so she was indoors a lot. But I was a tomboy, almost like a son to my dad. Even though I grew up in town, he raised me outdoors; and besides hunting and fishing, he taught me how to play sports. My parents never missed my games, and my dad came to every practice to watch and give me pointers on how to do better.

In the summers I traded in my sports uniforms for a bathing suit. My very best memories growing up were spending time with my family at my grandparents' fishing camp, where I swam, fished, and water-skied in Lake D'Arbonne; climbed the pine trees that ringed the lake; went out in the bass boat; and enjoyed fish fries and campfires.

Papaw and Mamaw Strickland, my grandparents on my dad's side, owned a fishing camp at Lake D'Arbonne. Outside his trailer Papaw kept an old horizontal freezer, unplugged and full of dark, crumbly dirt and earthworms. I spent lots of time, just for funsies, digging around in the freezer for worms. I loved the feel of the cool, damp soil and didn't at all mind the dirt under my fingernails.

When I got tired of the worms, I'd head down to the little beach and go swimming or lie on the warm sand as the boats went in and out. I learned how to water-ski on my Tweety Bird skis and later how to slalom. Mom refused to go in the warm, brownish water. She was girly and didn't like to get her hair wet. It never failed, though, but Dad would pick her up and throw her in the lake, kicking and screaming.

As I grew older, my parents let me invite friends to the lake. After swimming and fishing, we'd sometimes take walks along the water and down to the woods, where we'd pick up arrowheads. I remember exploring old, abandoned shacks—half there, half not—that captured my imagination as I wondered what delights awaited inside. I began to find joy in discovering and rescuing abandoned treasures, such as hundred-year-old dishes, left behind and waiting for someone to come along and give them a new home.

Not only did I love the campfires, fish fries, and time spent with family and friends, but I really loved spending time with my grandparents. When he wasn't working on the oil rigs, my papaw was always around because he loved being with my grandmother, Lola. They were best friends and did everything together, including hunting and fishing.

Papaw had kind eyes and a little scratchy stubble on his cheeks that tickled when I gave him a kiss. He also had hair in his ears, and it was my job to help him trim it. He chewed tobacco from a little white bag and always kept a gold spittoon nearby. Papaw loved to sit around in his blue coveralls (the only thing I ever saw him wear) and shoot the bull with the boys. On Mamaw's deathbed, she made us promise to make sure he always had clean coveralls.

I'll never forget my mamaw's sewing room, filled with scraps and bolts of cloth, buttons, thread, and trimmings. In that room I felt like a little kid in the most beautiful toy store you could imagine, full of magic and possibilities. Mamaw kept busy making beautiful clothes and quilts, some of which I still have.

My dad followed his father into the oil business, starting out as a rough-neck and later becoming a supervisor. I was born in Bossier, Louisiana, before Dad's work took us to Shreveport, Louisiana, and later to Tyler, Texas. Eventually, we ended up back in West Monroe in time for me to attend first grade.

When we relocated to West Monroe, we moved into an apartment building. One day a little girl named Meredith, with dark, curly hair and freckles, knocked on the door. "Want to play?" she asked.

Did I ever! We quickly became best friends and attended first grade together. She loved ballet, tap, and jazz, the complete opposite of me. In elementary school I was all sports and nothing feminine.

My mom was a teacher and also worked in real estate. Both my parents worked hard, but we didn't have a lot of extra money. I never felt poor because my mom was a clean freak—everything was always spotless—so I thought our house was awesome. Mom never left dishes in the sink and never went to bed with dirty laundry still in the hamper, even if it was just half a load.

Saturdays were for deep cleaning the house. My mom, sister, and

I would get up and clean on Saturday mornings while my dad washed the cars. Sometimes after the house was clean, my mom would treat my sister and me to dinner at Red Lobster, where I loved the cheddar garlic biscuits. We'd always buy a dozen to take home for snacks. After our dinner out we sometimes would go shopping for a new top and, on occasion, a whole new outfit.

Even as a young girl, I was drawn to beautiful fabrics and intricate designs while on those shopping expeditions, but it would be years before I started sewing and making things myself.

––––––––

Although I loved being outside, I was also obsessed with babies, just as I am now. I loved my Cabbage Patch dolls and their sweet, round, dimpled faces. I also had tons of Care Bear stuff. My dad knew how much I loved babies of any kind, and one Easter he brought home two little bunnies, one dyed pink and the other purple. I also wanted a baby monkey and begged my parents for one. I never gave up hope that someday they'd surprise me with one, but they never did. Later, though, I worked for a summer in the baby nursery at our local zoo, taking care of two baby ruffle tailed lemurs named Laurel and Hardy, each about the size of my hand. Dreams can come true!

I never cared much for indoor pursuits, such as board games or books or video games. I would always rather be out riding four-wheelers, climbing trees, or playing baseball in the yard with the neighborhood kids. But since my mother was a teacher, I also liked to play school with my friends. Mom would give me her extra papers, and at the end of the year, she let me have her bulletin board, full of numbers and letters and maps of the states. I had my own little corkboard, and I'd put assignments up for Meredith or other neighborhood friends. Sometimes I helped Mom prepare her classroom for the upcoming year by washing the desks with shaving cream and wiping off the chalkboards with a damp rag.

I wasn't a straight A student, but I tried my best, and I never wanted to get in trouble or disappoint my parents. Even though I was friendly and a talker, I followed the rules and tried to make sure everyone was happy with me. Mom always asked that I be seated in the front of the room because I was easily distracted. Usually if I sat in the front, I would do well. I liked math best and didn't have to try too hard at it.

In second grade I had a teacher named Miss G who seemed like the meanest lady in the world. I was scared to death of her. One day in the car on the way to school, I blurted out to my mom, "I just wish Jesus would come back today."

"Why?" she asked, wondering what had brought this on.

"So I don't have to go back to Miss G's class!"

I realized later she was just a stricter kind of teacher trying to keep control of the class, but since I always wanted everyone to love me, I took it personally. At the end of the school year, she asked me to be a flower girl in her daughter's wedding, so I guess she really did love me after all.

I never wore a Rocky robe; instead, I was usually in a blue leotard or some other sports uniform. I entered the world of competitive sports for the first time when I started gymnastics in second grade. My best event was the floor exercise. I was more athletic than graceful and could do a lot of flips. My weakest event was the bars. I later played basketball and softball, ran track in junior high and high school, and participated in cheerleading.

I loved sports because I liked spending time with my dad, but I also liked the team camaraderie, and my teammates were like my sisters, all rooting for each other. I enjoyed winning, but I wasn't the type to cry or throw a fit when I lost. I played my best and enjoyed the challenge of going after my dreams. Sports kept me from being bored and getting into trouble since I didn't have time for distractions. Participating in sports also meant being with other people, and I made new friends wherever I went.

FOUR

Pistol Pete

Jep

> When I was in the eighth grade, all I wanted to be
> was a great basketball player like my dad.
>
> —from the movie *The Pistol*

PETE MARAVICH WAS ONE OF THE GREATEST BALL HANDLERS THE NBA ever saw. And after I watched *The Pistol,* a movie about his eighth-grade year playing high-school varsity basketball, I wanted to *be* him.

A former professional basketball player who became a college coach, Pistol Pete's dad started him on the fundamentals of the game when he was only seven years old. For the next few years when he wasn't in school, Pete spent his time doing ball drills and practicing passes, head fakes, and long-range shots. At the age of eleven, he once made five hundred free throws in a row. He went on to star on the Louisiana State University basketball team and then moved to the

NBA to play for the Atlanta Hawks and the New Orleans Jazz. He averaged forty-four points a game in the NCAA and was one of the youngest players ever to be inducted into the basketball hall of fame. Pete got his nickname from shooting the ball from his hip, as if he was pulling a gun out of a holster.

After I watched *The Pistol* about a hundred times, and *Hoosiers* about fifty times, my hero Rocky Balboa got pushed aside. I shed my blue bathrobe and picked up a basketball instead. Dad had put up two basketball hoops on big trees out front. I spent hours every day practicing, just like Pete. I could just barely put the ball up to the rim, and I always had to wait until my brothers were done before I could start.

Since I was the little brother, I was a benchwarmer when Willie and Jase were playing ball with their friends. But when it was just me and Willie, sometimes he'd get down on his knees until we were about the same height and play basketball or football with me. (That's when he wasn't scaring me by telling me he saw a tiger in the woods. I completely believed him, but somehow I never saw the tiger for myself.)

I had already tried football because I wanted to be like my dad. In the 1960s, he was the starting quarterback at Louisiana Tech, ahead of the legendary Terry Bradshaw, who sat on the bench. Dad was born with a great arm. In high school, he used his strength to throw footballs, pitch baseball, and throw a javelin, making his mark on all three sports. I loved sports, too, but while Dad was six foot three, I was super short and not the average quarterback-kind-of-guy. But watching Pistol Pete convinced me to try basketball. I remember coming home from elementary school and practicing ball-handling drills and shooting baskets until bedtime. I was determined to be a great basketball player.

But even though I was excited about basketball, I was still a kid growing up on the river, and I loved to fish, hunt, and play video games.

Our house was small, just two bedrooms, one bath, a kitchen-living room combination, and a laundry room. My parents had the master bedroom, Jase had the second bedroom, Willie moved himself back into the laundry room to have some privacy, and I didn't have a room at all, so I slept on the couch in the living room.

I didn't much mind the living room—it meant I was closer to the television and my video games. I started with Atari, a gift from Mom and Dad, and played the heck out of *Pong* and *Donkey Kong*. I had the original Nintendo, the first edition, where you had to insert the game cartridge, move it to the sweet spot, and apply just the right amount of pressure, or it wouldn't play. Once, when I was about ten, I had chicken pox and had to stay home from school. I spent the whole week playing *Mike Tyson's Punch Out*, and toward the end of the week, I finally beat Mike Tyson. I ran outside hollering and jumping for joy. All of a sudden I felt better and had so much energy, I even ran down the driveway to get the mail for my mom.

I also loved my couch bed when Christmas rolled around. Every Christmas Eve I would go to sleep with one ear and one eye open, listening for Santa. Mom would come put out the presents, and she'd prop up a pillow to block my vision, then watch the pillow for any movement from me. For years it worked, and I believed in Santa Claus until middle school. Somehow Santa knew how much I loved action figures and always took the time to set them up in elaborate action scenes under the Christmas tree.

I kept the faith in Santa way longer than most kids, becoming sort of a Santa defender.

"There is no Santa. It's really your parents," kids would say.

"You just don't believe," I'd calmly explain. "It wasn't your parents putting out the toys until you quit believing."

But the moment of truth came, even for a believer like me. One Christmas Eve when I was about eleven or twelve, I was asleep on the couch when I heard a noise. I peeked around the propped-up pillow, careful not to knock it over, and I saw Mom setting up wrestling action figures inside a little toy wrestling ring. I watched as she took each one out of the package, being extra careful not to make any noise with the plastic, and then set up the action figures inside the ring to make it look like the wrestlers were going at it, just like on TV. That's when I had a revelation. *It's Mom who's been doing this the whole time.*

I also loved my He-Man and GI Joe action figures. When my brothers got too old for action figures, they switched to collecting baseball cards. I was in heaven when I inherited all of their He-Man figures, one of the few times they did something nice for me. I was more used to being ignored out front when they were playing with their friends or having my head shoved into a toilet. Another favorite torture Willie used on me was shoving my face into his sweaty armpit after he played basketball.

One time, I'd had enough of the armpit routine, and the only way I thought I could get him back was to go into his room and mess with his beloved baseball cards. I snuck back to the laundry room, tiptoed under the "I'm surrounded by idiots" sign above his door, found his box of baseball cards, and used a pair of scissors to turn them into confetti. I'm sure I must have destroyed some pretty nice cards. I got three licks from my dad later, but it was worth it.

Dad had a spanking system he had developed and refined on my three older brothers. He didn't have a lot of rules—he could sum it up as "Don't act like idiots"—and he relied on us to have common sense and learn by watching and doing. He also expected us to respect him as our father and to respect the Lord Jesus. But he needed some guidelines; so he gave us three rules, counted off on three fingers:

1. Do not ever disrespect your mother.
2. Do not hit your brothers.
3. Do not wreck or disrespect tools or hunting equipment by leaving them out or dirty or by breaking something. (Dad had been a commercial fisherman and now put food on the table by hunting and fishing, so his nets and guns were more than just entertainment or a hobby.)

Breaking any one of those three rules resulted in an automatic three licks on the butt from Dad's belt. Not only did the lickin' hurt, but the waiting was even worse. When my brothers or I were guilty of violating one of the rules, he'd say, "Go to my room, go to my closet, get out my belt, put it on the bed, and sit there. I'll be there in a minute."

That minute sometimes stretched into ten, fifteen, or even thirty minutes as he finished whatever he was doing, calmed down from his anger, and waited for the thought of what was coming to sink into us good and deep. I knew he was doing the licks to teach us how to behave, and I always respected him.

To be honest, though, if Dad was really unhappy, the three licks could turn into what we called a "syllable" whipping. In between licks, he'd say, "I. Can't. Believe. You. Did. That!" I would always cry. My dad's a big dude. But he'd always say "I love ya" and quote some scripture about training or discipline.

The worst whipping I ever got involved Willie and Jase, who knew how much I hated olives. We were having some sort of family get-together when they decided to hold me down and see how many black olives they could shove in my mouth. I was trying to get away and causing a ruckus when Mom heard and came in.

"Jep, why are you going crazy?" she asked.

"Shut up!" I yelled. I really didn't direct it at her, more at my brothers who were all talking and trying to explain why they'd been sticking olives down my throat, but it didn't matter. I knew I was in big trouble for disrespecting my mom. I ran down to Granny's and hid under the bed.

"Where's Jep?" I heard my dad's voice booming a few minutes later. Boy, he whipped me for that one.

As I got older, when it came time for a lickin', I came up with a new plan.

"Just let Mom do it," I'd tell Dad. Sometimes he'd agree if he was busy. Then I'd go get the belt and sit and wait for her.

When Mom came in, I'd beg her not to spank me.

"I'll do the dishes for a month," I'd plead. Being softhearted, she sometimes gave in. To cover for me, she'd grab Dad's belt and start to hit the bed with loud thumps.

"Ouch!" I'd yell. "That hurts, Mom!" We'd fake an entire spanking, and then I'd come out with tears in my eyes so my dad could see. We never told him about our deal, and to this day, he still doesn't know. *Sorry, Dad.*

Mom was very warm and loving. My favorite moments with her were spent in the kitchen, helping her make biscuits or chicken and dumplings. She would use our time together to share life lessons or talk about the Bible. She always had time for me. She used to take me with her to deliver food to some of the hungry people around our part of the river.

"We're all just people," Mom would say. "Every race, every color, we all have the same blood."

We used to take garden vegetables to a woman who lived nearby. She'd had eighteen children but was older now and very poor. Mom knew I was still young, and she was worried about what I might say, so she tried to prepare me in advance.

"Look, her stuff's going to be different, so don't make a big to-do about it."

When I walked into the older woman's rickety house for the first time, I noticed she had a bed sheet hanging in the kitchen doorway instead of a door.

"That's pretty," I said, pointing to the sheet-curtain. Mom looked at me, raising her eyebrows. I ran through it a couple of times, pretending I was a superhero busting through a wall.

Next, I noticed her old-fashioned rotary dial phone.

"I never saw a phone that color before," I said. Mom held her breath, nervous. "That's pretty," I added.

Mom gave the woman the food we had brought, and as we left, I didn't want her to think we were going to forget her.

"My mom's going to bring more stuff. She's got lots of it," I volunteered. I think I made my mama proud and didn't embarrass her too much. She always says I have a tender heart and that my oldest brother, Alan, and I are most like her.

While Dad was a tough disciplinarian, I knew he loved me too. He isn't much for hugs, but I hug him often. I'm the only one of my brothers to hug him and call him "Dad." And even though he didn't like to come to my school activities or my basketball games, he did take me hunting, starting when I was small. Mom would bundle me up to fight off the damp Louisiana cold that sinks deep into your bones, and Dad would take me along to the duck blind. He built a little step so I could see out, and as soon as I could, I started taking shots. I'll never forget shooting my first duck. Unfortunately, it was illegal, and we ended up with a gun being pointed back at me.

FIVE

Biscuits and Sugar Syrup

Jess

Cooking is love made visible.

—Anonymous

SUNDAYS WERE ALWAYS MY FAVORITE DAY OF THE WEEK. NOT ONLY because of church, although I went to the Pentecostal church every Sunday with the women in my family. No, it was the Sunday spreads on Mamaw's table that captured my heart.

Every Sunday we headed to Arcadia, Louisiana, where my mom's parents, Papaw and Mamaw Fincher, lived. Papaw Fincher worked at the chicken plant in Arcadia, and he often brought home a bag of chicken hearts as a treat for Mamaw, who would flour them and fry them up, like chicken nuggets. Papaw loved to work in his vegetable garden, and whatever Mamaw didn't use for canning, pickles, jellies, or salsa, he would sell at a little stand by the side of the road.

Papaw was also somewhat of a gambler and loved to go to the races.

He even ran a little bookie business on the side, but don't quote me on that (especially since police officers used to stop by the house sometimes to place their bets).

Every Sunday, my mom, dad, sister, and I would make the forty-five minute drive to my grandparents' home to have breakfast. On the menu were homemade biscuits with sugar syrup, fried eggs, bacon, and sausage. Huge country meals, made with love, covered the table, and around it sat my family—mom, dad, grandparents, aunts, uncles, and cousins.

After breakfast we went to church. For lunch we enjoyed a second big Sunday feast usually involving fried chicken or deer meat, fresh peas or corn, garden tomatoes, and homemade hot-water cornbread or fluffy yeast rolls, mixed up and kneaded the night before.

After lunch my cousins and I would play in my grandmother's backyard, pushing each other on the swing, climbing trees, running around, chasing each other, and exploring the small country town of Arcadia where my mom grew up. Arcadia is in Louisiana's beautiful Piney Hills country, surrounded by lakes. It's known for great deer hunting and for being the place where Bonnie and Clyde were killed. Arcadia has a cute little downtown area of one- and two-story old brick buildings with covered overhangs, and it was fun exploring the streets lined with antique shops and barbecue joints.

The town, and Mamaw's house, were happy and peaceful, always there and always the same. As a child it was comforting to know that as soon as Sunday was over, I could look forward to another Sunday in Arcadia at the beginning of the next week. Sometimes during the summer, I would stay for a couple of weeks. I loved sitting on the porch swing with Mamaw Nellie on warm summer evenings, eating popsicles. We'd eat three or four apiece. Another thing I loved to do was roast marshmallows over the gas flame on her stove.

I learned the secret to a really good fried egg from Mamaw. First, you fry bacon in a cast-iron skillet, then pour the bacon grease into a nonstick pan. Next, use a really good spatula to fry an egg in the bacon grease, taking care not to break the yolk. Delicious! But as good as I got at making eggs, they were never as good as Mamaw's.

––––––––––––––

We've always been a close family that likes to eat together. My mom is a big dessert maker, and one of my favorites is her homemade cheese-cake with graham cracker crust. She's one of the few people who has mastered homemade beignets. And around the holidays Mom made the best homemade divinity and fudge. She was really artsy about Christmas cookies, and we'd always make cookies for the school's cookie competition. The holidays centered on food and being together with family—cooking in a warm kitchen and snacking all day, with a fire crackling in the fireplace.

Mom has always loved being a girly-girl and keeping a perfect house. I'm not sure my mom actually could have handled having a son. My grandmother tells a story about my mom as a little girl. She had a fluffy rug and wouldn't allow anyone to step on it and create a footprint. So of course her brother, my Uncle Steve, made it a point to step on it every day out of spite. It made her so mad.

Mom grew up without much money, but when she was in high school, she saved her lunch money for the week, five cents a day, and used it to buy a honey bun. She's always had a sweet tooth, and she says that honey bun was always the best part of her week.

Even though I was a tomboy, my mom taught me I could be strong, competitive, and athletic, and still be a lady. She was okay if I wanted to be silly and funny and burp like a boy at home. But not in a restaurant.

"You need to act like a lady," Mom would say.

When I was young, she helped me pick out the right clothes and taught me how to do my hair. She wanted my sister and me to look nice, and I never took our shopping trips for granted. I knew she was choosing to spend her money on those special times with my sister and me.

We had a pretty small house back then, but we always had food on the table and didn't lack for anything. I don't remember ever comparing what I had, or didn't have, to other people. Once my parents splurged on a trampoline for us, and I thought, *This is awesome. We're rich!* But of course we weren't. My parents both worked hard and spent plenty of money on me—my uniforms, trips, shoes, and other sports expenses were planned for and paid.

Even though my dad acted as though he didn't want any animals, he continued to surprise me with pets, like the pink and purple rabbits. One day he came home with a big smile and said, "Jess, go get that big box out of my truck."

I had no idea what was going on, but I went and looked in the truck, and there was the cutest little boxer puppy. He was white with black spots, and his name was Max. We also had an energetic black Lab named Bullet. And when I was a senior in high school, Dad bought me a Pomeranian at Bonnie and Clyde Trade Days in Arcadia. She was the cutest thing ever—a furry puffball in a light cream color.

I continued to try hard in school, always trying to raise my Bs to As or my Cs to Bs. But I worked even harder at sports. I wanted to be good, and I don't ever remember Dad saying I couldn't do something just because I was a girl. He worked hard trying to make me better on the ball field. On weekends he would throw with me, or we would go to the batting cages to practice my swing, and I appreciate that because I learned how to work hard.

I did feel some pressure at times because Dad did have a temper and would yell at me during some of my softball drills. When I was about ten, I took a year off from softball but decided I wanted to go back the next year. Dad coached my softball team all the way through elementary school. He was tough on me—no favoritism. I can still hear his words ringing in my ears, like "keep your eye on the ball," and "swing level." I wanted to do well, and I didn't want to be out there giving less than 100 percent. I wanted to be the best I could be.

Whenever I had a little extra time or just wanted to relax a bit, I'd watch old TV shows: *I Love Lucy*, *Laverne & Shirley*, *Three's Company*, and *The Dick Van Dyke Show*. I loved Doris Day movies, and I listened to country music singers like Garth Brooks, Clint Black, Reba McEntire, and the classics—Loretta Lynn and Patsy Cline. I've always been drawn to vintage and classic, whether it's music, movies, or fashion.

Probably the hardest moments I had growing up were the occasional tense times in my parents' relationship. I remember crying and wanting everything to be the same, to be peaceful and safe and routine at home between my parents. But, as in most marriages, there were some emotional struggles, and my parents didn't always get along. That might be one reason I became so involved in sports—it was an escape, and it was stable.

Church with my family was another positive element in my life. But even though I went to church every Sunday, as a child I was afraid of God's punishment if I disobeyed, and I felt anxious about being good enough to get into heaven. I always felt God was real, and I believed in Jesus and was conscious of Him all the time. I knew He saw everything. So I tried hard to live in the way God wanted me to live.

I thought I was a Christian because I didn't do some of the things my friends did. I thought faith was all about works—what you did or didn't do. I was a church girl to the core, raised in a Christian environment with lots of rules and expectations. But somehow I missed learning about the love of Christ and, even though I loved Sundays and going to church with my mamaw and my mom and aunts, it was so hard to be perfect.

Between church, school, and sports, I worked harder and harder as I got older, and I never wanted to let anyone down. Whether because of family, teachers, coaches, or friends, I started to feel pressure to always do everything just right. My desire to please grew, and it wasn't long before it seemed to control my life.

SIX

Ducks and Dogs

Jep

Anyone who does not provide for their relatives, and especially for their own household, has denied the faith and is worse than an unbeliever.

—1 Timothy 5:8 NIV

DAD STARTED TAKING ME OUT HUNTING WHEN I WAS ABOUT SEVEN. HE loved showing me how to hunt game and provide for the family.

"Playing sports only lasts for a short while," he'd say. "But as long as the woods and river are here, we can always find our food."

We hunted for ducks, turkeys, doves, squirrels, and deer—all high quality, lean, nutritious protein, organic, and hormone- and GMO-free.

I learned early on that killing was a small part of what we were doing out there. It was the getting up early, the wondering what the day was going to be like, the long trip out to the blind, and the time together with family and friends. I loved hearing the ducks calling in the distance and the rush of wings when they came in close.

Duck hunting season happens in late fall and early winter, and believe it or not, it gets icy and damp down here in Louisiana. We once had some guys from Maine come down and hunt with us on a super cold, twenty-degree day, and they swore it was the coldest they'd ever been.

The wet cold can get into your bones, especially when you're a little kid. One winter day, probably the coldest day that year, Dad and his friend Mac took me out hunting at a duck blind he'd built into a beaver dam down on the river. Dad could tell how cold I was getting, and he looked concerned.

Mac took one look at my red, windblown cheeks and blue lips and said, "Let's build a fire."

"In the duck blind?" said Dad. "There's no fire pit in here."

"He's really cold," said Mac.

"Okay. We'll do it," said Dad. And they did. They built a fire in the duck blind, and I sat close, took my boots off, and warmed my toes and my fingers. I was happy, and they shot a bunch of ducks that morning because freezing weather can mean awesome duck action.

Dad's method of teaching me how to hunt mostly involved taking me along, showing me how to take care of a gun, load it, and use it safely for myself and around others, along with how to call in ducks and bring them down. I was expected to watch and see what to do, and then to do it correctly.

I'll never forget my first real duck hunt because it didn't end up the way I thought it would. I was still pretty young, and I was hunting with Dad and Bill, who was the best friend of my oldest brother, Alan. Bill was around a lot and almost like an uncle or older brother—he really watched out for and took care of me.

At first, there was nothing to shoot. Then Bill said, "Hey, I know where all the ducks are. They're next door over at Jimmy Don's. I'm going to take Jep over there and see what's going on."

"Be careful," said Dad, "because that's not our property and we're not supposed to be over there."

"We're just going to take a look," reassured Bill.

Bill and I gathered up our guns and gear and took a boat down the river and over to the neighboring property to scout out the duck holes. There were ducks everywhere. We'd found the mother lode of mallard ducks! My heart was beating hard. I wanted to shoot my first duck, and here they all were, right in front of me, ready for the taking.

Boom! I squeezed the trigger of my dad's shotgun at a mallard drake flying by and folded him up. I was so excited when he dropped into the water. My first mallard! It was a big deal, and I felt grown-up and knew my daddy would be proud of me.

Just as I was getting ready to wade into the water and get him, we heard a truck speeding down the road, getting closer by the second. Sure enough, up zoomed Jimmy Don in his old truck. He jumped out and ordered, "Put your guns on the ground."

I was terrified and speechless, shrinking back into my jacket and hood, hoping he couldn't see my face. He knew my family and my dad for sure, but I wasn't sure if he knew me. And he definitely didn't know Bill.

"You're going to jail, boy!" he shouted at Bill, wiggling the gun for emphasis.

Bill started talking fast. "Hey, I didn't know this land was posted," he said. "I didn't know we were doing anything wrong."

Jimmy Don just stared. I kept my head down.

Then Bill had a bright idea. "My son just killed his first mallard drake," he pleaded, waving over at me. I could see his leg quivering although he was trying to act tough.

"You're going to jail," answered Jimmy Don.

"We're not here to have some kind of gunfight," said Bill. "I'm sorry. Can my son go get his first mallard? It's right there. We can see it from here," he continued, pointing over at the duck floating on the pond. I looked up out of my hood, hopeful.

"No!" shouted Jimmy Don. "You're going to get off my property, and you're lucky you're not going to jail. But since it's his first duck, I'll let it go."

I was about to pee my pants in fear, but ole Jimmy Don took pity and finally let us go without pressing charges. Maybe he just meant to scare us away, but the whole incident didn't take away the excitement of killing my very first mallard. I have to admit, I didn't picture looking down the barrel of a shotgun when I imagined my first duck hunt. In the end, though, I still thought it was the coolest day ever.

Dad wasn't too happy about it. "You all were just supposed to go scout," he grumbled.

Dad has always said we're not rednecks; we're river rats. With the river just a few feet from our front door, we were out almost every day either hunting or fishing the river, the creek, and the beautiful calm bayou, all connected. It was a lot of fun, but there are a lot of hazards too. In West Monroe we are blessed to have all four indigenous poisonous snakes: water moccasins (or cottonmouths), copperheads, Eastern rattlesnakes, and coral snakes. Several of our dogs have been bitten by snakes. Our black Labrador retriever, Blue, got bit in shallow water by a water moccasin. His skin rotted around the bite, the vet had to remove a big chunk of his chest, and he narrowly survived with a big scar as a souvenir.

Another time I was in a boat and saw a water moccasin swimming toward the boat. I started shooting into the water and finally hit him right before he reached the boat. I don't know if he would've slithered in or not, but he sure acted as if he was on a mission to get really close.

Somehow none of us kids ever got bit, but a snake did end up helping create a nice scar on my calf. I was fishing for catfish with a couple of buddies when we saw the snake. We thought it was a cottonmouth, panicked, and started running. In the excitement I dropped my pole and then tripped over it. Instantly I felt a sting on my leg and thought it was the snake, which only made me run faster. When I looked down, I saw the eye of a fishhook, not a snake, buried deep in my calf. As I ran, dragging the pole behind me, the big catfish fishhook burrowed even deeper. I stopped and started yelling. My buddy grabbed the pole but didn't have a knife to cut the line.

All this happened on a Sunday night, when my parents had house church. About eight couples were in the house with my parents. My other buddy ran to the house. I could hear him yelling: "Jep's got a hook in his leg!"

Dad came out from the house, along with everyone from house church, to see what the fuss was all about. "Well, don't he make a little production of it," he said, looking at my leg with the fishhook sticking out of it.

He calmly produced a pair of pliers, cut the line with the nippers, grabbed the tail end of the hook, and pushed it forward into my leg. He couldn't pull it straight back out because of the backward facing barbs. He steadily guided the metal hook through my calf and up and out of the wound while I screamed and yelled. He finally got the eye of the hook through and out. Then he pulled out a bottle of rubbing alcohol and doused the wound, causing more yelling.

Dad isn't really fond of doctors. He has lots of home remedies so he can avoid having to be treated by a medical professional. Besides alcohol, there's Campho-Phenique, his cure-all for bites, rashes, and anything and everything. Sore throats are treated with a grandma's hot toddy made of bourbon. Dr. Tichenor's Antiseptic is a favorite disinfectant; we call it "Dr. Tish's." And then there is Monkey's Blood, or Mercurochrome, which is what Granny poured on all open wounds.

Besides snakes and fishhooks, we had to watch out for the river itself. Mom and Dad were not the kind of parents to hover over us and track everything we did. We pretty much just went and played in the yard and the woods and did whatever we wanted. It might be considered lax compared to parenting today, but I loved it. It was a *Goonies*-style childhood, filled with exploration and adventure.

But my parents did have a few safety rules, and the first one was, *If you can't swim, don't get near the water without someone who can swim.* Now, my parents don't swim—I don't think I've ever seen my dad swimming even though he was always on or in the water. They didn't teach me, and I think they just expected me to gradually learn on my own. But as I got to school age, I still didn't know how to swim. I did feel safe in Dad's boat, though, and I knew he'd take care of me. He made me wear a life jacket most of the time.

One day my buddy Chess was over, and we were hanging out. Carl "Chess" Streuben was my best friend and the only person my age on our road.

"Let's go down by the water," said Chess.

I wasn't wearing much in the way of clothes. When I was really little, I liked to run around naked, a lot like my Uncle Si when he was a kid. During my Rocky robe years, I often just wore the robe, nothing else. Mostly I just tried to wear as little as I could get away with. On this day, I think my only article of clothing was a pair of tighty-whities.

One of Dad's hunting dogs, an older black Labrador retriever named Gabe, tagged along with us. Gabe was a big, powerful, barrel-chested dog. We went out on the pier, where Dad kept his boat and nets, looked around, and decided to throw sticks for Gabe. We went back up on shore, gathered some sticks, and walked back out on the pier.

Chess threw his stick first, and Gabe jumped in, swam out to get it, then swam back to the pier and climbed out, ready for more. I threw my stick next, trying to fling it farther out on the water. We kept throwing sticks, and Gabe kept fetching them. He was such a powerful swimmer he created his own little wake when he swam.

Chess and I competed to see who could throw the stick farther, and pretty soon we were getting a running start the whole length of the pier and chucking the sticks like javelins. And that's when it happened. I started at the back end of the pier with my stick, ran the whole length, and somehow I couldn't stop at the end. My speed and momentum carried me out into the water, and I fell in with a splash. The cool water gave me a shock as it went over my head. It wasn't too deep, probably only about six feet, but I was only about three feet tall.

I immediately panicked, flailing my arms and legs as I bobbed to the top like a cork. Chess took one look at me and turned around and ran for the house. He could tell I was in trouble.

I was thrashing my arms and legs and gasping for air. Within seconds I was coughing and choking as I swallowed river water. Just then, I felt a whoosh of energy pushing water toward me, and there he was. Gabe! Good ole faithful Gabe had swum and grabbed the stick I'd thrown, and now he was paddling his way back. He came straight toward me, and somehow I had the presence of mind to grab his collar.

You would think a panicky, drowning kid grabbing a dog in deep water would drag the dog down underwater, but not Gabe. He was swimming with such power and strength that he continued on his way back to the pier, even with me thrashing around.

When he got close to the pier, I grabbed on with one hand and then let go of Gabe and hung on for dear life. I wasn't strong enough right then to climb out, so I just hung on the pier for a bit. I was dazed, but I finally started trying to pull myself up and onto the pier. That's when Chess and Dad arrived on the scene. I was unceremoniously jerked up by the arm, still coughing, crying, and gasping as I tried to fill my lungs back up with air. Dad patted me on the back a few times, trying to help me breathe. His face was white, and he looked freaked out, and he never freaks out.

When he could tell I was going to be okay, he snapped out his first words. "Son, you're about to get your butt tore up."

I remember that being a particularly painful spanking. I was wet. My rear was wet. And the belt hurt. But after that, I paid special attention to the rule.

SEVEN

Up Early and Workin' Hard

Jess

Growing up, I wanted desperately to please, to be a good girl.

—Claire Danes

I'M NOT ONE TO SLEEP IN LATE, AND I NEVER HAVE BEEN. EVEN IN JUN-
ior high and high school, when most kids stay up late and sleep in as
long as they can, especially on weekends, this was my schedule:

9 p.m.—asleep
6 a.m.—awake
6:45 a.m.—at school

I made it work by creating routines. I had a job my senior year and
worked Monday through Saturday. I usually didn't go out at night, so
after dinner I'd take a bath and pick out my clothes for the next day.

I had my own bedroom with a sleigh-style daybed. I set up a desk and created a little office for myself to do homework. At first, I had an old desktop computer, but I hated to ask for money for extras, so I saved my own money, and one Black Friday I got up super early to stand in line at Walmart to get a new computer at a great price. I was never a big poster person, so instead, I decorated my room with bulletin boards loaded with pictures from cheerleading, sports, and camp. I also had my trophies, megaphone, and letter jacket on display.

In the mornings, I'd get up, take a quick shower, throw on my clothes, do my hair, and put on a little makeup. I didn't wear a ton, usually just some powder and mascara on my top lashes. I skipped breakfast and within moments was out the door.

My schedule worked best when I started driving myself to school after I got my driver's license at the age of fifteen. (Kids learn to drive early in the South!) My first car was an old, white Mercury Cougar with red velvet interior and automatic seatbelts that buckled you in when you started the car. I knew it was ugly, but I didn't care because I loved having a car.

I enjoyed seeing my friends at school and felt comfortable in all different kinds of groups. I got voted onto Homecoming Court twice. As a freshman homecoming princess, I wore my sister's old prom dress since we didn't have a lot of money. In my senior year, Meredith nominated me, and I didn't even know it until I won.

I always had lots of guy friends, too, because they were easy to talk to and not as emotional. I always felt like girls were a lot of work. But I did have three best girlfriends who would hang out with me: my old friend Meredith, Casey, and Laurie. During the midmorning break at school, my friends and I would usually head to Chick-fil-A for a chicken biscuit or to Shipley's for a fresh glazed donut, right out of the fryer.

I had a lunch allowance from my parents, but at home I would make a turkey sandwich for lunch, bring it to school, and save my allowance. I was always careful with my money. My first jobs were babysitting for kids in the neighborhood, and I started a savings account and put a lot of what I earned away. Starting in fifth grade, I babysat for our next-door neighbor, Debbie. She had two sweet girls, Hailey and Hannah. Debbie owned a stylish boutique in West Monroe called Herringstone's, which carried classy but fun and funky clothes. I eventually started working there, kick-starting my lifelong love of fashion. I'd always been picky about what I wore, but working at Herringstone's moved me up from shopping at The Limited and introduced me to the next level of fashion and accessories, and I loved it. Herringstone's is still there on Forsythe Avenue in Monroe, and I still shop there.

Through junior high and high school, I continued to work hard in school and tried to make good grades. I was good at math and science but had to work harder in English. At first, I wanted to be an attorney when I grew up. I have a strong sense of justice and right from wrong, and I like to win. I also hoped I'd be able to make a good living—I knew I didn't want the money struggles I'd seen my mom go through in her work as a teacher. But I would've been the worst attorney of all time because I'm too emotional. I probably would have cried all the time, especially when I lost a case.

Later on I wanted to be a CPA, which appealed to my love for organization and numbers, but I was probably too energetic and too much of a people person to be stuck away in an office with a stack of spreadsheets.

Most of my school days ended with a sports activity, such as gymnastics, softball, basketball, track, or cheer. I didn't last too long in track—I ran hurdles and relay and was fast at short distances but hated any kind of long-distance running. I was better at softball, where I played left field.

Cheerleading dominated my high school years. I loved the discipline, the sense of community, the energy, and the excitement. I liked doing flips and stunts in the air and getting the crowd pumped up. And I loved that we were a team, and it wasn't just all about one person. I was proud of the West Monroe Rebels. Our football team played in the state championship every year at the Superdome down in New Orleans, about a five-hour drive from West Monroe. It was one of my favorite times of year, with the streets full of people in Rebels sweatshirts and hats. All of the parents were involved, positive, and encouraging.

My parents never missed a game and always went along to New Orleans for the big game. They had tons of friends among the other parents, and they seemed to enjoy it as much as I did. My dad was always my number-one fan. As I came into my teen years, I began to realize that my dad's motorcycle accident, which put him into a full-body cast back when he was a teenager, had cut his own athletic career short. Money had been tight in his family, too, so his opportunities had been limited. This realization helped me understand a little more about why he'd been so enthusiastic about my playing sports, starting with signing me up for gymnastics when I was in the second grade. But over time sports became more about spending time together.

On weekends, when I wasn't babysitting, I'd sometimes hang out with friends, both girls and guys. We'd go to ball games or out to the lake for water-skiing. Sometimes we'd go mud digging—we'd drive out in trucks or Jeeps or four-wheelers and look for big mud holes (and there are many in Louisiana). We'd drive through, splashing the muddy water everywhere and trying to get stuck, and sometimes parents had to be called to pull us out. If school was closed due to stormy weather, we headed straight for the mud holes.

I still went to church every Sunday with Mamaw, in Arcadia, and for a while I casually dated a boy who lived there. His mother was my mom's best friend. He was a year younger than me and very nice. I'd drive over by myself to see him and to see my grandmother. Sometimes I'd stop by the old cemetery in Arcadia to read tombstones. I liked seeing the names, reading the dates, and trying to figure out who these people were and what their stories might have been. It didn't feel scary or spooky at all. Somehow it made me more conscious of life and death, what's really important, and in high school I started to think about God in a more grown-up way.

My friend Casey invited me to go to youth group at her church in West Monroe. I discovered I knew some people from school, and I started going regularly to youth group on Sunday nights and Wednesday nights. I still visited Mamaw Nellie on Sundays but came back for youth group in the evening.

During my freshman year of high school, I was pretty serious about a different boy. He was super cute and a football player. He made me laugh, and I fell hard for him. Ninth grade was a great year, and I finally felt like everything was going my way. I was doing well in school, enjoyed cheerleading, and felt happy and loved. My boyfriend and I started talking about getting married someday, and my future seemed bright and full of romance.

But then reality hit. During cheer camp the summer before tenth grade, I heard rumors about his cheating on me. I finally found out that the "quarterback who's dating a junior high girl" everyone was talking about was actually *my* boyfriend. I had no idea, and it seemed like everyone had known but me. I was devastated. In every cheer camp picture that year, you can tell my eyes were swollen from crying all night long.

At that time, I didn't have a cell phone so I had to wait until I got home from camp to talk to him. When I confronted him and told him what I'd heard, he didn't deny it. All he said was, "I know." There was no apology and no remorse.

I was devastated. The rejection and his uncaring attitude changed everything for me. My heart was more than broken, it was crushed, and it sent me into a downward spiral of self-hating thoughts and emotions.

Am I too ugly?

Am I too fat?

If only I was prettier, skinnier, and smarter, he'd still love me.

For the first time in my life, I felt not good enough, not pretty enough, and not thin enough. I'd always been a confident child, super involved in sports and everything else, but my gregarious nature changed all at once. The breakup did a lot of damage to my pride and my self-image. I felt like I'd discovered I wasn't who I thought I was.

I began to isolate myself, and for the next couple of years, I didn't date anyone seriously. I started working more hours to stay busy and tried to forget what had happened. In my heart of hearts I was hoping that somehow we'd get back together. Even though he had cheated on me and thrown me aside like a piece of garbage, I believe I would have gotten back together with him if he had asked. But he didn't.

My withdrawal continued as I stopped hanging out with my friends and even quit softball and cheerleading. I knew Dad was disappointed—he'd worked hard to instill a love of sports in me and had spent so much time trying to help me improve. He was worried I was throwing it all away for nothing, and I hated feeling like I'd let my father down. I went from being an outgoing, confident girl to a broken, insecure recluse.

After the breakup, Dad tried to cheer me up by buying me a car to replace the old, white Cougar. We went to a few car lots together and looked at cars. I wanted a Jeep, but he was afraid I would flip it over. A used white Ford Mustang convertible caught my eye. It had a khaki-colored top and interior.

"Okay, I like that Mustang," I said.

I was joking—I never thought he'd buy me something like that, but the next week he surprised me with it. My parents had always been pretty frugal and careful to make ends meet, but I think he could tell the breakup hit me hard, and he wanted me to have something nice. Dad could've used his money to buy himself a new car or a boat, but he loved being able to buy me the Mustang and was proud he could afford it.

Soon my excitement over the car wore off, and I started beating myself up again. I worried about my looks, and I began to obsess on my weight. Always, in the back of my mind, was this dark thought: *I'm not good enough.*

And that's when the eating disorder started.

EIGHT

Brothers, Basketball, and Bucks

Jep

I smile because you're my brother. I laugh because
there's nothing you can do about it.

—Unknown

MY BROTHERS WERE AROUND WHEN I WAS SMALL, BUT AS I GREW UP,
they were busy with their own friends. When they were around, I was
mostly off to the side, watching them play basketball or fish or get
ready to go hunting. They did teach me a lot, though.

Alan, my oldest brother, was out of the house doing his own thing.
He's more like an uncle or a father to me—he used to take me along
on some of his dates with Lisa—and he has always been a wise advisor.
He knows pretty much everything I've ever done.

I've leaned on my brother Willie a lot for guidance too. He's honest and tells me what I need to hear but not always necessarily what I want to hear. Willie is the funny one. He's always on, and he can make any situation funny—even the serious stuff. I look up to my brother Jase as a man of integrity and honor. He's also the best duck hunter, next to my dad.

I'll never forget when my brothers took me out frogging for the very first time. (Frog meat is like a mix between chicken and fish but super tender.) When we would go frogging, we'd leave the house at ten or eleven at night and didn't come in until daylight. It was late for a little kid.

We never caught them by giggin', which is spearing frogs with a long-handled metal fork. Giggin' wasn't dangerous enough, I guess. Instead, a real man grabs the frog with his bare hands, or at least that's what Jase always says.

You go out in a boat and use a powerful spotlight to shine in the frog's eyes. When the frog is blinded by the light, he freezes, paralyzed. If the spotlight man is good and steady, then you just run up quick in the boat, lean over, and grab the frog on the way by.

I was in charge of the ice chest, where we stashed the frogs. When one of my brothers caught a frog, he'd hand him over to me still alive, and I'd stick it in the ice chest. After serving as ice-chest man until about two in the morning, I was worn out and fell asleep right on top of the ice chest.

I have another good memory of Jase, riding around with him in his truck one day when I was about ten or so. He had his string of duck calls, and he would pick a call and blow it.

"What is that?" he'd ask.

It was a whole lot of fun, but he was serious too. He made me close my eyes and not look at him while I listened and then made a guess.

"Gadwall?" A gadwall call uses both a whistle and a reed.

"No." Jase blew the call again.

"Mallard?" I guessed.

"Drake or hen?" he asked.

Female ducks, even if they're the same species, always sound different from the male.

"Hen."

"Right!" Jase said, blowing it again to help me remember for next time.

Besides the different breeds of ducks, such as mallard, teal, pintails, and wood ducks, there were drake and hen, and flying or sitting on the water. There was a lot to learn, and the cab of his truck was duck-call school.

My brothers and I also worked together helping Dad with the fishing business, which he was still running as he got Duck Commander off the ground. I'd drive the boat, Willie and Jase would help pull in the nets, and then we'd go with Mom to the fish market to sell fish. We were starving by dinnertime. I remember Mom setting out fried chicken and my brothers calling "breast!" or "drumstick!" and sometimes I'd get left with the neck, so I learned to fight for my piece and eat fast. I also remember Mom letting us have the good pieces, and she'd take the leftovers.

———

There were plenty of times when I drove my brothers crazy, just by being a little kid. When I was about eight, Willie moved a cot to the laundry room and claimed it as his room. Jase had the second bedroom, and I still slept on the couch in the living room. The problem with Jase's bedroom was you had to go through it in order to get to the bathroom.

One day Jase came in and crashed in his room for an afternoon nap. I was on the couch and needed to go to the bathroom. I crept through his room, trying hard not to make a peep, but he's a light sleeper, and I woke him up accidently. Half asleep and mad, he picked up his alarm clock and threw it at the back of my head. *Bam!* It took me by surprise and just about knocked me out. I started crying, Dad heard it and wore Jase out with the belt on his behind.

Willie did his fair share of little brother torture too. In addition to his sweaty armpit trick, he used to drive like a maniac. He had this ugly orange Ford Mustang with white vinyl seats, and he drove super fast on the back roads leading out to our house.

"Do not tell Mom I'm driving like this," Willie warned me one day.

"Okay, I won't," I said.

And I didn't. That day. But before long he started picking on me, and I knew just what to do.

"Mom!" I yelled.

"What do you want, Jep?" she answered.

"Willie was driving really fast, and he didn't want me to tell you." Sweet revenge.

When Jase got married, Willie moved out to the old red shack on our property that Dad had used to clean fish and claimed that as his own, so I finally got my own room and didn't have to sleep on the couch anymore. I was about ten years old.

Right about that time we had a big surprise from Granny. It was close to Christmas, the weather was nice, and I was outside, following Willie and his buddies around while they played football in the yard. Then we heard some gunshots nearby. *Pop! Pop! Pop!*

It took a while for the noise to get our attention, but after a few more shots, we began to pay attention. It was Granny, out in front of her house, holding a .22 rifle. As I watched, she pointed it at our house and squeezed the trigger again. *Pop! Pop!*

"She's shooting at the Christmas lights," someone yelled.

I started laughing, not believing what I was seeing. We all ran up to the house, shouting, "Granny is shooting at the lights!"

I was good and excited; I thought she was just having fun. But Dad took it much more seriously. He immediately burst out of the house and marched straight up to his mother.

"Ma, you're gonna give me this gun right now," he said. "My kids are playing out here."

My dad's serious expression scared me, and I realized she wasn't just playing; something was wrong. Granny was on meds, and they helped, but as I got older, I heard more stories about the crazy things she had done when her manic depression got the best of her.

Although we cut up a lot at home, my brothers and I behaved ourselves at school because our parents demanded it. The teachers, maintenance people, administrators, and bus drivers always bragged on us, telling our parents, "Your boys are perfect gentlemen."

We always answered our teachers with, "Yes, ma'am" and "No, ma'am." Dad used to say even if a teacher was mediocre, she was still the teacher, and we'd better do what she told us.

Dad always kept his advice simple. I remember riding home with Dad after church on Sundays, and he'd always say, "Now, son, you've heard the stories about when I was a drunk and mean to your mom."

He'd look over at me, his eyes serious. "Now, you're never going to be like that, right?"

"Yes, sir," I'd respond. And that was it. We probably had that exact exchange a hundred times while I was growing up.

I began to like school a little more in fifth grade when I became friends with my principal, Mr. McCall. He was a big baseball-card collector and owned a card shop in the old part of town. Willie and Jase used to trade cards with me but always ripped me off, trading me four worthless baseball cards for a great card, like a Rickey Henderson rookie card. But Mr. McCall was very fair with trades, and I ended up with some awesome cards.

I was a pretty good kid in middle school. And I started liking school even more when I got good at sports. I started out playing flag football because I wanted to be like my superstar quarterback dad, but I was never really into it. Plus, I was smaller than Jase and Willie. But I loved basketball. And because I practiced so hard with the basketball hoop on that tree in the front yard, I could shoot, and it didn't matter how big I was. I became a shooting fool, doing my own drills, dribbling, and shooting until dark every day. When it was cold, I'd go inside and hang out with Granny and watch *Murder, She Wrote*, which I still love to watch.

By the time I made it to junior high school, my hard work had paid off. I was a stud, averaging eighteen points a game. I would shoot hundreds of three-pointers until nine or ten every night, my arms and legs worn out. Mr. McCall was also my basketball coach, and he taught me about hard work. I owe a lot to him. He played me at point guard and told me, "No matter what, son, you put it up. If you can shoot it, shoot it."

Pinecrest Middle School was a small school with about twenty in my class, so I had lots of game time, and in sixth grade, I played on the eighth-grade team. Mr. McCall's confidence in my ability, plus my hyperfocus on perfecting my three-point shot, helped build my confidence. Mom came to all my games, and Willie came to some too. He coached the seventh graders the year I was in eighth grade. In one of my best games, I made nine three-pointers. Even though we were playing much bigger schools, some of them ten times our size, we won a few games. We got beat on pretty good, too, but I still felt good about my game.

I watched basketball a lot at home and became obsessed with Michael Jordan. I joined the Michael Jordan fan club and saved up money from my chores to buy Michael Jordan posters and key rings out of his monthly newsletter. Anything associated with Michael Jordan, I had to have. By middle school I was begging Mom for Michael Jordan shoes.

By the time I graduated eighth grade, the duck call business was beginning to make some money, and my parents decided to put me in Ouachita Christian School, where my dad had once been a teacher. It was the first time they could afford private school, and they wanted me to have a good education and stay out of trouble. I made good grades and tried out for basketball. I took it very seriously and made the team but quickly realized I wasn't top dog anymore. I wasn't quite the stud I thought I was, but I still loved to play. I didn't have the best freshman year, so I trained extra hard that summer because I still wanted to follow in my dad's footsteps. Even though football hadn't been a good fit for me, I was hoping to get a full basketball scholarship to college.

While basketball had a strong hold on me, I still loved hunting, and I had my first deer kill when I was thirteen. I'd been with Dad on a few deer hunts and watched carefully. As I said before, he wasn't one to explain a lot. "You watch me and see how it's done. Eventually, you can go and get your own deer," he'd say.

One December I got up early on a super cold morning, the temperatures down in the twenties, with heavy winds and sleet. Mom didn't want me to go out deer hunting.

"It's way too cold," she told my dad. "He's going to be all by himself. This is a bad day to do this."

I had an old 30/30 rifle for deer hunting. Guns are expensive, and I didn't get my own, brand-new shotgun, a Remington 870, until I was fourteen years old—as a Christmas gift. Before that, I used my dad's guns, and he used Pa's old Browning A5, a semiautomatic, sixteen-gauge shotgun.

"They don't make 'em anymore because they're too good," Dad would say.

Jase came over at 5:30 that morning, and he and Dad took me to the deer stand, basically a drafty, wooden box on stilts with a couple of windows to shoot out of. Mom had given me a big sleeping bag to take to the deer stand so I could keep warm. Dad climbed up on the box with me and gave me a sort of pep talk, telling me to aim behind the shoulder. Then he and Jase left.

The blind was freezing cold and dark inside, and I was all alone and kind of scared. I unzipped the sleeping bag and wrapped it around me. Within ten minutes I was dead asleep on the floor.

Dawn broke, and two and a half hours later, I finally opened my eyes. *Oh, my goodness. I've been asleep a while.*

I pushed the sleeping bag off and stood up to peek out the window. Right in front of the deer stand were two deer—a doe and a small four-point buck (legal back then). My heart started beating hard in my chest. I grabbed my gun and eased the old rifle up onto the ledge.

Then I squeezed the trigger and *boom!* The buck fell right over while the doe took off. I was so fired up.

I climbed down the ladder, dragging the sleeping bag with me, and sat down by the dead buck. With no cell phone, I just sat, wrapped up in the sleeping bag, and waited for my dad. And, yes, I fell asleep again, right next to the warm body.

"Son, get up." A voice penetrated my sleepy head.

I jumped up and wrestled my way out of my warm cocoon.

Dad was there, and he was excited too. He's not a big hugger, but he patted me on the back. "You got one."

I smiled up at him.

"I can't believe you just laid down beside him, though."

"Sir, I got tired and lay down and went to sleep."

"Gotcha. Well, he's a good one," Dad said.

NINE

Pressure

Jess

You are imperfect, permanently and inevitably flawed. And you are beautiful.

—Amy Bloom

LIKE MANY PARENTS IN THE SOUTH, MY PARENTS WERE PRETTY STRICT. Since Mom was a teacher, she was tough on me in terms of my education. Dad was strict on my activities; he wanted to know where I was going and who I was going with and what time I'd be home.

I never really got in much trouble with them, though. I didn't like to get in trouble, so I tried my best not to. I can only remember getting a few spankings. More often I'd watch my sister get in trouble, and I'd think, *Okay, I'm not going to do that*.

My Mamaw Nellie spanked me once. I'd told my sister I hated her, and my grandmother found out and told me to go outside and pick a switch.

"You never tell anybody you hate them, especially your sister," she said.

She spanked me, but she cried more than I cried. It really did hurt her more than it hurt me.

But as strict as my parents were, I was much, much stricter on myself. After my heart was broken, it was as if my competitive spirit turned inward, and I began to compete against *me*.

My senior year I quit sports—I didn't cheer or play softball. Instead, I worked, and I worked hard. I had early dismissal and was out of school at 10:30 every morning, headed straight to work. I continued to work at Herringstone's, and when I wasn't there, I was babysitting. I saved almost every dime I made except for buying some clothes. I loved working in the fashion world although it did make me feel as though I had to be thin, like all the models I saw.

I thought the girls around me were prettier, and I started drastically cutting back on calories and working out harder and harder. I used a calculator to track the calories I ate and sometimes made a meal out of just a few marshmallows or a bowl of low calorie cereal.

In the South, delicious home-cooked meals are supposed to bring the family closer. I'm sure my family must have noticed that I was not only counting calories at the table but also eating very little. I cut out butter and then any kind of fat. I wasn't starving myself to death or making myself throw up, but I began to realize I had a problem when I went to one of my favorite places, Piccadilly Cafeteria, with my mom, and there was absolutely nothing I felt I could eat. The cabbage seemed to be drowning in butter, and I couldn't force myself to eat it or any other vegetable on the buffet. Every single thing seemed greasy. I wanted to enjoy a meal with my mom, as I had since I was a little girl, but I just couldn't seem to let go and enjoy the food. I was a person who liked to do everything right and maintain control, but in the process of trying to be perfect and look perfect, I had actually lost control of my eating. My eating, or lack of it, was now in control of me.

During this time, when I was hurting from a lack of confidence and heading into what seemed to be an eating disorder, I became more and more involved in youth group at church. Since I wasn't doing cheer or sports, which had been such a big part of my life, I turned to youth group as a place to hang out with Casey and other kids my age. With working every day, I felt pretty grown-up and seemed to be losing the carefree, outgoing part of me.

At church the youth minister always seemed to smile and pay special attention to me, which made me, and my hurting heart, feel better. One summer day between junior and senior year, he called me into his office and shut the door.

Maybe he's going to ask me if I can help with a special project or do some work with the younger kids, I thought. I waited, happy that he had noticed me. I was ready and willing to do whatever he asked. I wanted to help.

He smiled. "One of the girls told me you liked me."

What?

Well, of course I liked him. He was my youth pastor. He was friendly and fun and liked spending time with all of us. Youth group was a safe place to hang out and learn about God and about life. So when our youth group leaders acted as though they liked us, it made us happy.

"I want you to know I feel the same way about you," he added, looking more serious.

I felt unsure and a little scared. On one hand, hearing those words made me feel good. *I can't believe this godly man likes me. Maybe I need to like him back.*

He seemed like a really honorable guy. I remembered all the times he'd spent with us, energetic and staying up late and playing games with the teens in the group. And he *was* kind of cute.

But he was older, in his midtwenties. And I was only seventeen years old. I didn't know what to say back or how to react. I think I was in shock because I hadn't expected him to say those words. Being around him had felt safe, up until now.

"I think we should keep this between us," he said, more serious now. "We need to wait until you're eighteen and out of high school before we tell anyone we're dating."

And that's how it started. I didn't realize it at the time, but that twenty-minute conversation in his office changed the course of my life. As I walked out of his office, I felt extremely confused. Part of me liked the attention of a man I respected as a man of God, a leader in the church, and someone we all liked to spend time with. In a way, I felt almost like Cinderella, being picked by the prince. *He really likes me*, I thought. For a girl who didn't feel good or thin or pretty enough, it was a powerful feeling to be noticed and chosen. I felt special.

We secretly started seeing each other. He'd call me, and we'd hang out around his office at church or at the senior pastor's house, where he lived. They all seemed to know about our relationship and seemed fine with it. But it was hard on me, having this secret relationship, and I began to separate myself from everyone who was close to me. I did whatever he told me to do and started to become a loner.

On November 12 of my senior year, I turned eighteen years old. I was at school the morning of my birthday when a family friend, who had been like a father to me, had me called into the office. *Is he delivering some flowers from my dad? Or checking me out to take me to a birthday lunch?* But when I walked into the office, I took one look at him, and I could tell something was wrong.

"Your mom's been in a bad car accident," he said.

"What do you mean?!" I immediately told myself she was going to be fine, but in reality I was in shock and didn't want to think too much about how bad it could be.

When I got to the hospital, I learned Mom had been on her way to school that morning when she was broadsided by a big truck. Her car spun around and hit a light pole, breaking all her windows. The glass went everywhere, including into her ears and mouth. She was rushed into surgery.

When she came out, her face was swollen, and I couldn't even recognize her. I'd never been through anything like this and was scared when I saw my big, strong dad cry. I realized it was serious. Over the next few months I had to grow up a lot and help take care of Mom. My dad stepped up and helped out too.

Mom eventually had several surgeries to put a rod into her spine to hold it all together. She was in the hospital for a couple of months then went through rehab to learn how to walk again. She suffered a lot of pain, and it was a while before she could stand for any period of time. While she was recovering, I became more and more independent. I worked until five every day, including Saturday, and went to church on Sunday. I didn't spend much time with friends—my life began to revolve around work and my new, somewhat secret boyfriend.

Now that I was eighteen, we became a little more open about our relationship. Some of the girls in youth group were mad when we started dating, almost as if they were jealous. At one point we had an argument, and I broke up with him. I remember one girl saying, "You're so lucky he likes you."

I thought, *Well, maybe they're right, and I should get back together with him.*

I also started to feel that I should be in love with him even though I wasn't in love with him. I wanted not only to please him and make him happy but also to please the people at church, who seemed excited that we were dating. Even my parents seemed happy that I'd found such a wonderful man. Everyone said I was the luckiest girl in the world to have snagged him.

The longer we were together, the more I began to feel the pressure growing. He came to my high school graduation in May and seemed excited and happy that I was now a high school grad. Now there were fewer distractions. When I wasn't at work, I was with him.

One day he asked me how many men I had slept with.

"None," I answered.

He seemed surprised. Although he had never been that physical with me, he admitted he'd had a wild few years before he became a youth minister.

About a month after my high school graduation, we were at the beach on an outing with my family when he dropped to his knees and produced a ring. "Will you marry me?" he asked.

I was excited. I suddenly felt very grown-up and ready to leave my parents' house.

"Yes," I said right away and gave him a hug and a kiss. I ran over to my parents and excitedly showed them the ring. They seemed happy for me. They knew I wanted to be a wife and a mom. I still loved babies, as I always had, and I looked forward to becoming a mom for real, instead of a babysitter for someone else's children.

He pushed for a quick wedding, so we decided to get married in December. My life sped up and became a whirlwind of work and wedding plans. But a big part of me felt more and more scared, alone, unsure, and confused.

Do I really love him? Is this what love feels like? Am I ready to get married?

Whenever I shared any of these thoughts with him, he'd say, "It's going to be okay. It's God's plan for us to get married."

TEN

Things Fall Apart

Jep

Disappointment is a sort of bankruptcy.

—Eric Hoffer, *The Passionate State of Mind*

ON SUNDAY NIGHTS, DAD AND THE HOUSE CHURCH MEN WOULD SOME-
times take me trot-lining with them. We'd take a couple of boats out
and string out the long trotlines, weighted at both ends with plastic
milk-jug floaters in the middle and multiple baited hooks. My dad
knew just where to go. We'd catch all kinds of fish, but the best were
the big Opelousa cats. We'd bring whatever we caught back, and
Dad would clean the fish and cook them. He's a great cook, and the
men loved it.

But Dad did more in the river than just fish. He also baptized
people. Men and women who were in trouble somehow found their
way down to our house, where my dad and mom would stop what they

were doing and talk to them. In our living room is where I first started to realize that there was something to this God stuff my dad was always talking about. These people would come in looking like they'd been down a long road and were worried, unhappy, unhealthy, and just plain scraggly. Dad would talk to them about God and Jesus as I was sitting there on the couch, watching and listening. Pretty soon he'd take 'em down to the river and baptize them. I'd see them later, singing at church, but they looked different—happier, healthier, changed from someone you might run away from to looking like the nicest person you've ever met.

There's something to this, I began to think. I knew God was real, but there was something powerful happening with the words my dad was using out of the Bible. And my dad not only shared Jesus with people, but he also helped people. Mom and Dad always took people in—vagrants, criminal types, and people with mental problems. Word got around. If people had a cousin or a friend in trouble, they'd offer Dad up: "There's this guy who lives down by the river. People come to see him. He can help you."

It didn't matter where you came from or what you were like. Dad would welcome you in and talk to you. People have compared him to John the Baptist, baptizing people in the river. With the hair and the beard, he even looks the part, and he played the part of John the Baptist in a play at church one Christmas.

I took all this in as a little kid, not completely understanding it all but still soaking it in. One day a friend of mine, a boy named Harvey, came to visit. We were sitting in the backseat of the car while my mom drove when I asked Harvey if he'd been baptized. When he said no, I started telling Harvey what was going to happen when we got to the house.

"When we get there, my daddy is going to open his Bible and start preaching, to tell you all about Jesus and how He died on the cross and rose again and how He's coming back to get us."

Harvey seemed to be listening, so I kept going.

"Daddy will talk for a long time and tell you everything you need to know. Then he'll say, 'Harvey, who is going to be the Lord of your life?'"

Harvey looked at me, his eyes big.

"The answer is Jesus Christ," I said.

Harvey nodded.

"When you say that, my daddy's going to take you down to the river to be baptized."

He looked a little nervous.

"It's a real deep river, but you won't drown. Daddy will baptize you in the river, and then we'll go away. Everyone will be happy, and then we'll get dry clothes on."

I was a little disappointed when I realized Harvey was young and not quite ready to make Jesus the Lord of his life.

I also saw my parents live out their faith in real time as they took people in to our house. It wasn't unusual for people to be living with us while they tried to get their lives straightened out. Dad ran a little boot camp of sorts, taking people hunting and fishing and showing them how to do good honest work, in between nightly Bible studies. Sometimes we even had people sleeping on the floor. I saw what it meant to really love your neighbor. Once, Mom went to the mental ward of the hospital and picked up one guy who had asked for help.

"What would you like to do with your life?" Dad asked him.

"I want to drive a big rig," he said.

So Dad spent time with him and helped him, baptized him, got him into trucking school, where he earned his certificate, and then sent him off down the road to make his way.

Several years later, with no warning, a massive red eighteen-wheeler truck rumbled down our long driveway and stopped in front of the house with a honk. The guy who'd been in the mental ward climbed out of his rig and stood proudly on the running board. He was hauling a load of chickens and had stopped to show off his rig to Dad. He was married, working steadily, and had turned his life around with my parents' help.

I listened to Mom and Dad, watched what they were doing, and saw what a difference God made in these people's lives. When I was thirteen years old, I told Dad I was ready to be a Christian, and he baptized me in the river too. I loved church, loved the Bible lessons, and had good friends there.

When I was fifteen years old, I experienced a powerful answer to prayer. I worked out so hard for basketball and had all the normal aches and pains of athletes who push their bodies to the limit, but I began to experience a different, terrible pain in my abdomen, and I was afraid to tell anyone about it. Plus, I didn't want to miss basketball.

During practices my stomach would really hurt. It got worse and worse, and soon it was becoming hard for me to even walk. My abdomen below my belly button started bulging out, and I often had to lie down because the pain was excruciating. I really thought something serious was going on and I was going to die. I just didn't know what it was and was afraid to tell anyone. I started praying and praying hard: "Lord, don't let me die," I begged. "I'm too young."

When my basketball coach finally noticed I couldn't run or jump, he took me aside.

"Son, is something bothering you?"

I knew he wouldn't let it go, so I finally told him what was going on. "You have to tell your parents," he said.

I knew the coach would tell them if I didn't, so I did. When she heard, Mom took me to the doctor and found out it was a simple hernia that could be repaired with a quick and easy surgery. I was so relieved. I took it as an answer to my fervent prayers. With God's help, I made it through what was a very big deal at the time.

I loved God, and I loved learning about Him and His Word, but the further I got into adolescence, the more church became about me and about meeting girls, not about God.

While I was interested in girls, I was also scared of them and had never had a girlfriend. I remembered some of the rough girls from the school bus when I was a kid and shuddered. I thought girls were gross, and I didn't want to be around them. Dad used to say, "Girls will steal your heart and break it," and I wasn't sure I could really trust a woman with my heart. Plus, I was definitely shy. I tried to act as though I was cool, but I really wasn't. I'd acted like a big dog, but I was more of a nerd. At home, when I wasn't practicing basketball, I read a lot of books. I loved to read, and I think I read every Louis L'Amour book there was.

Finally, though, I met a nice girl the summer of my junior year and had my first real girlfriend. She was a good influence on me and kept me out of trouble. I spent a lot of time with her family, and because we were always together, Willie teased me by calling us the "twin-headed dragon."

Spending time with my girlfriend kept me from obsessing on basketball as I did when I was younger, but I still worked really hard, both during the season and off-season. Early in high school, I had worked hard and become known for being a good up-and-coming ballplayer. I was small but fast, and I thought of myself as more of a jock than my brothers. Mom still came to most of my practices and games. Dad came once or twice but didn't like coming to town, so he missed a lot of my games.

Then, with no warning, everything fell apart. The summer before my junior year, I was playing in a scrimmage. The game was really close. I got the ball and took the shot, just like Coach McCall had always told me. I jumped high and released the ball, but something happened when I came down. Maybe I was too focused on watching the ball arc toward the rim, but when I came down, my left foot turned slightly in, and all of my weight pounded down onto my left ankle, and it snapped under the pressure. When it broke, it sounded like a rifle shot. I collapsed on the floor. Everyone in the gym stopped what they were doing and ran toward me.

"Are you okay?" my coaches and teammates asked.

I was trying not to cry with the girls around, but I sure wanted to. It hurt more than anything I'd ever felt. They carried me over to the bleachers, and I asked for some water. My ankle started swelling up, and my mom raced into town to pick me up and take me to the hospital.

We waited what seemed like forever in the emergency room, but I was eventually admitted. The news was not good. X-rays showed a break; plus, I'd torn all three ligaments. It couldn't have been any worse. The doctor said I would be in a cast for at least three months, and after that I would need physical therapy to get my strength back. He wanted to do surgery, but Dad always says, "The last thing you ever want 'em to do is cut on you," so we turned down the surgery.

The doctor warned me that I might not be able to walk right again, but I decided to take my chances and try to heal on my own. I was discharged with painkillers, crutches, and a cast and hobbled to the car. As I rested over the next few days, reality began to set in. If

I couldn't jump or run or maybe not even walk, I wouldn't be able to practice basketball. If I couldn't practice, I wasn't going to be able to play on the team my junior or senior years. If I couldn't play basketball, I wasn't going to get scouted by colleges, and I wasn't going to earn a scholarship. My basketball career was over. Maybe it had all been a pipe dream, but it had been on my heart for so many years.

In a split second, my life changed completely. My basketball dreams were crushed. I no longer had anything to work for. No more practices, scrimmages, or games. No more drills at home or three-point-shot marathons until dark. My freak accident not only destroyed my ankle, it destroyed my identity and everything for which I lived and breathed. I was going to have to reinvent myself. And that's when everything started to go bad.

ELEVEN

It's Too Late

Jess

I always put on a brave face when I was the most
terrified, the most trapped and out of control.

—Natalia Kills, 2013 DigitalSpy interview

MY DOUBTS GREW STRONGER. SOMETHING WITH THIS RELATIONSHIP
just didn't feel right. I wasn't sure I loved my fiancé the way a wife
should love a husband. Any physical attraction I had felt was melting
away, and I was starting to feel trapped. I wanted a way out, but I didn't
feel I could break it off because I didn't want to upset him, and I didn't
want to upset the people at church.

The only person who really seemed to understand what was going
on was my sister. Stacy had gotten married the year before to a guy
she met in nursing school named Andy Austin. It had been a beautiful
country-club wedding, and I loved my peachy pink maid-of-honor
dress. I saw how their marriage was so full of love and admiration for

75

each other. Stacy and Andy were best friends, but I knew I didn't feel the same way about my fiancé.

At one point during my engagement, I ended up at my sister's house, crying. "I don't know if I want to be married to him," I sobbed. "I don't think I'm ready."

She listened, and her house felt like the only safe place I could share my true feelings.

"You need to go to him and tell him how you feel," she said.

Of course Stacy was right, but that was just about the hardest thing she could say to me. I had a difficult time being honest about my feelings because I didn't want to make anyone unhappy. But I was beginning to feel desperate, and somewhere I got the courage to talk to him.

"I don't want to be married," I told him. "I don't think I'm ready."

"You can do this," he said with great feeling, almost like he was coaching me in a softball game. "You'll be great. I know you can do this!" He wasn't mean or harsh about it, but I couldn't seem to stand up to him and stop the wedding train.

When he could tell I was still very uncomfortable, he set up a meeting for me with an older woman who was known as a prayer warrior in the church. I shared with her how I felt, that I wasn't ready for marriage and I wasn't sure this was the right thing for me to do. "I'm not mature enough," I explained. And I really was starting to feel that—the earlier excitement about getting married had started to fade as the reality that I would spend the rest of my life with this man, who I wasn't sure I loved or was even attracted to anymore, started to sink in.

"Oh, you *are* mature enough," the older woman said. "You're scared, but that's normal." She patted my hand.

I wanted to throw up. I wish she could've understood the pressure I was feeling. I wish I could've shared my feelings more openly. It felt as if everything and everyone around me, except my sister, was pushing me toward marriage. I didn't feel as though I had anyone in my corner, and I couldn't seem to say no or stop something I knew wasn't right. I felt like a weak young girl, not a woman at all.

Wedding plans continued, and before I knew it, my wedding day had arrived. My heart wasn't in it, but I put on my dress and did my hair and makeup. I remember peeking out of the bride's room at the church and watching tons of people streaming down the hallway and into the sanctuary. I saw friends from high school, laughing and talking, and I wished I was with them, making plans to do something fun instead of being in my wedding gown about to pledge my life and my heart in a lifelong commitment to a relationship that seemed to have almost happened without me.

I didn't want to spend my life with him, or the next year with him, or even my wedding night with him. My chest felt weighed down by a ton of bricks, and I thought hard about running away and leaving it all behind. I wish I would have. But I was too immature. I felt helpless and hopeless.

I wanted to feel like the most beautiful and joyful bride in the world, but instead, I felt trapped and alone. I knew I had to go through with it. I didn't want to upset anyone, and I didn't want everyone at church to hate me. I was miserable.

I went back inside the bride's room to finish getting ready. I looked in the mirror, and all I could think was, *I can't leave. It's too late.*

Somehow within the space of a year, I had gone from an outgoing high school girl, who worked hard and loved sports, cheer, and people, to an isolated, confused, and unhappy young woman who could say no to food but couldn't say no to a marriage she didn't want.

I wasn't strong enough or brave enough to say it, so instead, I said "I do."

The wedding was a blur. So was my wedding night.

I was married one full year before I left. All of my friends were in their first year of college, and I was working on divorce papers.

During that year, I mostly kept the pain inside and built up walls around my heart. I wasn't sure I could ever let anyone inside again. My sister became very close to me during that time, and she seemed to understand what I was going through. I could really rely on her and felt safe spending time at her house with her and Andy. My marriage wasn't abusive, but I felt stuck and emotionally manipulated.

I knew I always had the option to leave him and go home to my parents, but the same pressures I felt during the engagement were still there, maybe even stronger now that I was not just a wife but a pastor's wife. I still didn't want to disappoint anyone, and I wanted to do what was right.

My financial situation was difficult, too, and I wasn't sure what to do. When we got married, I used all of my savings to help pay for the wedding and to put a down payment on our house. Not long after we married, he traded in my car, which I owned free and clear, and got me another car with a big loan attached. I quickly realized I didn't seem to have any say in our finances. I started working as a dental assistant and did earn a steady paycheck, but I wasn't able to save any of it.

Thinking about divorce was painful. I grew up in a very conservative Christian environment, where divorce didn't seem to be an option. I'd seen my mom and grandmother have their share of marriage struggles, but they never left their husbands. If they could stick it out, then so should I. But it was becoming clear that it couldn't work, and I eventually just gave up on the marriage.

Everything inside of me said I had made the biggest mistake of my life. I didn't want to spend my time blaming him when I could have said no or run away. I was a girl who was easily persuaded. I felt I had no voice, and I didn't even know what my own feelings were.

As I look back, I should have been stronger and braver. I should not have allowed myself to be pressured into the relationship or into an engagement and marriage. I should have run away, tried a different church, or gone to college. Things would have been different if I had reached out and found support—someone wise to be in my corner and help me figure out what I was doing and why I was doing it.

Many of us girls are easily persuaded, and we can get ourselves into difficult situations where we feel manipulated and silenced. *Don't let that happen to you. Reach out and ask for help.* If you notice someone who seems to be in that kind of trouble, make yourself available for support, guidance, and prayer. Look beyond the smiles and the "everything's okay" façade and really see the hurting, scared heart of a girl who needs your help to remove herself from a bad situation.

When I made the decision to leave him, I didn't tell anyone other than my family, and I just threw my stuff in some cardboard boxes and moved out on my own. I felt the whole situation was my fault, and I left him with the house, taking my car and car loan with me.

The last time I was at the house to pick up some things, he begged me to stay. I just couldn't do it. I'd made my decision, closed off my emotions, and hardened my heart; somehow that allowed me to leave. Then he said, "God will be with you. You'll meet someone else, and you'll be happy."

I didn't feel released or relieved, just numb—but that's how I had to feel in order to leave. I felt what I was doing was wrong, but I just couldn't do it anymore. My life seemed like it was over. *I'll never get married again*, I thought. *Who would want me now? I'll never get married, and I'll never have children, and I'll be alone the rest of my life.*

At the age of twenty, every single one of my dreams was dead.

At first, my mom was supportive and told me to come on home. But he wanted me back and began to work on getting my mom's support. She felt sorry for him and even gave him some money at Christmastime. So I hardened my heart a little toward my mom. It was my only way to get through it because I hurt so badly. I was ashamed and closed off, and I didn't know how to be honest with my parents or myself. I couldn't share with anyone at church either, so I stopped going to church at all.

I felt like the biggest failure in the world—at twenty I had already lost a husband, a house, the car my dad had given me, my church, my friends, my innocence, my dreams, and my future. I was lost and desperate, and I began to slip away from the world I'd always known and to take on a whole new life. My eating issues became worse. I started drinking and going to bars. And I started hanging out with the wrong people. It was almost as if I wasn't conscious of the difference between right and wrong anymore. I knew it. I felt it. I just couldn't stop the downward spiral of my life, and I didn't have anybody other than the fast crowd who welcomed me in and accepted me.

I began to do things I had never done. I felt pressure again, but this time even worse. I didn't like who I was becoming, but I still couldn't say no or disappoint people. Those three months after I left my marriage were the darkest of my life. The girl who never got in trouble became a lost girl who put herself in bad situations and let herself be taken advantage of in just about every way. I felt all was lost.

Just then, I went for a haircut, and on the way out of the salon, I walked by a guy named Jules Jeptha.

TWELVE

A Halloween to Forget

Jep

Habits are first cobwebs, then chains.

—Spanish proverb

WITH MY ANKLE AND MY BASKETBALL DREAMS SHATTERED, I HOBBLED into my junior year of high school. I felt more than a little lost without the routine of practices, games, and my own three-pointer drills at home. I didn't really know what to do with myself, and I started spending more time with my girlfriend.

She was beautiful and sweet and from a nice family, so everything was good for a while. But when basketball was torn away from me, I began to transfer my love of the game to love for my girlfriend. She became the object of my obsessive attention and my worship. I couldn't pay attention at church anymore—*she* was my church, and my world revolved around her.

I did have a few other interests. Even before I broke my ankle,

I'd started experimenting with some things I'd never done during my straight-and-narrow childhood. I knew right from wrong—my parents had taught me, and I'd been in Bible classes for years, so I had a strong conscience that generally kept me out of trouble. But by my junior year I'd started hanging out with a like-minded friend, and together we started cutting up. First, we started watching movies filled with sex and filthy language. I felt bad but got used to it really fast.

Then I started drinking. Beer came first. When I was younger, I never thought I'd be drinking. I don't remember ever seeing my parents drink at all. I knew very well what alcohol had done to my parents and their marriage before my dad gave his life to Jesus. My mom's mother had been an alcoholic; she died of sclerosis of the liver at fifty-eight. My older brother Alan struggled with alcohol and wild living for a season of his life before he became a pastor. And my brother Jase had been so scarred by seeing Dad's and Alan's struggles that he vowed not to drink a drop of alcohol ever, and he has never once been drunk. I knew all of this, yet I didn't care. I wanted to try it for myself. *I have to do it. It's just part of living*, I told myself.

The broken ankle and the loss of my basketball scholarship dreams led to more of this behavior and left me disappointed, angry, and with a bad attitude getting worse all the time. My girlfriend could see which way I was headed, and she decided she wanted out. We'd been dating for more than a year when she gave me the bad news—she was really sorry, but she didn't want to be with me anymore. I still remember that night. I begged her to change her mind; I pleaded for another chance. I tried everything and then cried my eyes out later. Somehow she knew I was turning into a bad dude, but I didn't care.

The breakup made me even angrier. *I thought we were going to be together forever, but I got nothin' now. No girlfriend. No basketball.*

I started going to parties and hanging out with people who drank and did all kinds of drugs. I was hanging out with my buddy one night when we decided to go to his brother's house for a party. He had a bunch of bottles, and we started drinking. I remember getting blind drunk and throwing up at two in the morning. After I finished and wiped my mouth, I started drinking some more. We drank all night and all morning, and then drove to school. I can't believe no one noticed.

Toward the end of my senior year, I started hanging out with an older group of guys who were already in college. They were involved in all sorts of things I had never been exposed to, drinking hard stuff, taking pills, and selling drugs. I had always looked up to these guys and thought they were so cool. I got curious and wanted to see if they were really having as much fun as it looked like they were having.

I remember the first time I got drunk with them. They took me to a party on a boat and started handing me drinks. I downed each one, and they kept on giving me more and treating me like I was the life of the party. I'd always felt a little awkward and had tried to cover it up by looking cool, but this time I really did *feel* cool. Everyone wanted to be around me, and I liked the feeling.

By the summer after graduation, I started trying drugs too. I smoked marijuana, took whatever pills were offered to me, whether I knew what they were or not, and stayed out all night long. I'm like my dad in that I don't do anything halfway. In the fall I enrolled at the University of Louisiana at Monroe (ULM) and moved with a roommate into an apartment. Things got worse because there was no one to answer to, so I started going out and partying every single night. I became real thin and unhealthy looking because the drugs killed my appetite.

One of the dumbest things I ever did was to try a wet daddy, a joint soaked in formaldehyde that had been stolen from a funeral home. We all sat around in some dude's apartment and smoked it. I didn't even know who the other people were, but it sent us on a trip. Whatever anybody gave me, whether it was a whipped cream can or a hit of LSD in some weed, I tried it. Even now, I don't know what pills I took. Whenever something new was offered to me, I remember thinking with the rational part of my brain, *It's probably dumb to do this, but they're all doing it. We'll be laughing about it tomorrow.*

At every party there was usually at least one person who'd be so drunk and so high that he'd get paranoid and start talking about the cops being outside. We thought it was hilarious. We always looked for the paranoid guy so we could make fun of him.

I was getting a paycheck from Duck Commander, but I wasn't showing up much to work or to my classes. My life revolved around the next party and the next chance to get loaded. On Halloween night of my freshman year in college, I went to a party and was doing the usual when I spotted a guy I knew. *Uh oh. I'm busted. That dude's in my brother's Bible study.* At the time, Willie was working as a youth minister down at the church, along with his job at Camp Ch-Yo-Ca.

I saw the guy was drinking, too, so I didn't worry too much about it. Then we all got real serious about getting stone drunk and taking a whole lot of drugs. The next thing I remember, it was morning, and I woke up sprawled on the side of a gravel road. I was cold, hungover, all skinned up with big bloody scratches, and lying on my back with one leg still hanging in the open door of my big green Chevy pickup truck.

Am I alive? What the heck happened?

I blinked my eyes, rubbed my face, and tried to force my foggy, hungover brain to remember what had happened the night before. I felt physically ill, and no one else seemed to be around. I had no idea how I got there or even how I could have driven when I was so out of my mind. *Was anybody in the truck with me? Was I in some kind of accident? Why am I out in the road?* I had no memory of what had happened. It was like a black hole in my mind, and I hoped I hadn't run over somebody or hit something.

At that point, lying on the side of the road like a strung out drug addict, I knew I had a problem and that my life had really gone off the tracks. But even though I was a mess, I dragged myself up off the road, climbed up in my truck, and drove home thinking, *When's the next party? Where're the drugs? Where's the alcohol? Let's keep rolling.*

The Halloween blackout had no effect on me. I didn't stop. I couldn't stop.

Pale as a ghost, I went down to about 150 pounds and looked pretty bad. The lies were dragging me down, and I felt empty, with nothing to look forward to. I lived for myself and had no decency whatsoever.

I did feel some guilt from time to time. I had to come up with a whole lot of lies to hide what I was doing from my parents and my brothers. I was still going to church every Sunday and working part time, when I was sober enough, at Duck Commander. I became a master at hiding my secret life and pretending everything was fine. My typical daily routine was wake up late, take a drink and smoke something, take a nap, wake up, and then do it all over again.

The Monday night after Halloween, I made myself go to the college Bible study Willie was teaching. There were about six or seven other guys, and we met in the gym. Brian, the guy I'd seen at the party, was there too. I wasn't too worried. Since he was at the party, he probably wasn't too proud of himself and wouldn't be telling my brother about it.

But Willie got up in front of us and said, "I know some of you guys are struggling, and struggling hard."

That got my attention. I didn't hear the rest of what he said, but I remember thinking, *He's never said anything like that before.*

A couple nights later, I got drunk and went to the movies. When I came out to the parking lot, I saw a note on the windshield of my truck. I picked it up and unfolded it.

"I know what you've been up to. We need to talk."

It was from Willie.

THIRTEEN

The Choice

Jep

Be on your guard! If your brother sins, rebuke
him; and if he repents, forgive him.

—Luke 17:3 NASB

THE NEXT MORNING I SHOWED UP AT DAD'S HOUSE AT EIGHT, WITH A
hangover. All my brothers' trucks were parked in front. *What are they
all doing here?*

When I opened the front door, Dad, Alan, Jase, and Willie looked
at me. They were sitting around the living room, waiting. No one
smiled, and the air felt really heavy.

I looked to my left, where Mom was usually working in the
kitchen, but this time she was still, leaning over the counter and looking at me too.

Dad spoke first. "Son, are you ready to change?"

Everything else seemed to go silent and fade away, and all I heard
was my dad's voice.

"I just want you to know we've come to a decision as a family. You've got two choices. You keep doing what you're doing—maybe you'll live through it—but we don't want nothin' to do with you. Somebody can drop you off at the highway, and then you'll be on your own. You can go live your life; we'll pray for you and hope that you come back one day. And good luck to you in this world."

He paused for a second then went on, a little quieter.

"Your other choice is that you can join this family and follow God. You know what we stand for. We're not going to let you visit our home while you're carrying on like this. You give it all up, give up all those friends, and those drugs, and come home. Those are your two choices."

I struggled to breathe, my head down and my chest tight. No matter what happened, I knew I would never forget this moment.

My breath left me in a rush, and I fell to my knees in front of them all and started crying.

"Dad, what took y'all so long?" I burst out.

I felt broken, and I began to tell them about the sorry and dangerous road I'd been traveling down. I could see my brothers' eyes starting to fill with tears too.

I didn't dare look at my mom's face although I could feel her presence behind me. I knew she'd already been through the hell of addiction with her own mother, with my dad, with her brother-in-law Si, and with my oldest brother, Alan. And now me, her baby. I remembered the letters she'd been writing to me over the last few months, reaching out with words of love from her heart and from the heart of the Lord.

Suddenly, I felt guilty.

"Dad, I don't deserve to come back. I've been horrible. Let me tell you some more."

"No, son," he answered. "You've told me enough."

I've seen my dad cry maybe three times, and that was one of them. To see my dad that upset hit me right in the gut. He took me by my shoulders and said, "I want you to know that God loves you, and we love you, but you just can't live like that anymore."

"I know. I want to come back home," I said.

I realized my dad understood. He'd been down this road before and come back home. He, too, had been lost and then found.

By this time my brothers were crying, and they got around me, and we were on our knees, crying. I prayed out loud to God, "Thank You for getting me out of this because I am done living the way I've been living."

"My prodigal son has returned," Dad said, with tears of joy streaming down his face.

It was the best day of my life. I could finally look over at my mom, and she was hanging on to the counter for dear life, crying, and shaking with happiness.

A little later I felt I had to go use the bathroom. My stomach was a mess from the stress and the emotions. But when I was in the bathroom with the door shut, my dad thought I might be in there doing one last hit of something or drinking one last drop, so he got up, came over, and started banging on the bathroom door. Before I could do anything, he kicked in the door. All he saw was me sitting on the pot and looking up at him while I about had a heart attack. It was not our finest moment.

That afternoon after my brothers had left, we went into town and packed up and moved my stuff out of my apartment.

"Hey bro'," I said to my roommate. "I'm changing my life. I'll see ya later." I meant it.

Later that day, after we talked more and things were starting to settle down, Dad said, "I'm going to put you on house arrest. You cannot leave this house for three months. You're going to study the Bible with me, and you're going to duck hunt every single day."

"All right, Dad. I think I can do that."

During the months I spent at Mom and Dad's, I hunted, fished, and studied the Bible every day with Dad. I began to realize that all this time, I had been living off of my dad's faith. I'd never had my own relationship with God. For the first time, I started to find my own faith.

As I looked at God's Word with fresh eyes, I realized that repenting and turning to God meant I was saved and forgiven. Jesus' blood covered my sins and redeemed me from the path of destruction I was on. I couldn't ever have been good enough on my own.

Back when I was in the middle of that crazy time of drugging and drinking, I remember feeling guilty once in a while and knowing I needed God. But then the thoughts would come. *I'm not good enough.* Or *I'm just not quite ready.* I think that's the number one excuse because you'll never be perfect, and you'll never be ready. Getting right with God and getting rid of the bad stuff in your life takes time. You have to take it one step at a time. It's not easy, I'm not perfect, and I still struggle.

Moving back home and starting to serve God for the first time, I cut all ties with my drug friends. I just turned my back on them. I knew I needed to change my habits and the way I'd been living, and I couldn't be around people who were smoking weed. I knew my dad's story—even after he gave his life to the Lord and was saved, he still struggled with drinking. It was a year before he could stop and a couple more years after that before he didn't want the alcohol anymore.

I didn't feel I could do it like that. I knew myself, and I knew I needed to do it all at once and stay away from bad influences. I knew I needed people to keep me accountable. I started going to a men's Bible study at church and making new friends. Looking back, I realized good guys were around me in high school that I could have hung out with. They were there. But I looked at them as a bunch of Goody Two-shoes and thought they were no fun. If I had chosen to spend time with them, I know I would've found God sooner and spared myself and my family a lot of pain. But I had different ideas back then.

My friend Trey came to know the Lord about this same time, and Dad allowed him to come to the house and study the Bible with us.

"How's your faith?" Dad asked him.

"I'm not sure it's all real," said Trey.

After we spent some time in God's Word, though, Trey was ready to make a decision to follow God, and after we prayed together, Dad baptized him in the river. My friend Gary was baptized that same night. Then Trey, Gary, and I started spending more time together. We were all on fire for God, so happy and grateful for His love and forgiveness, and we told the good news to everyone we came across.

I'll never forget one time we gathered up a group of more than a dozen old friends, girls and guys, and told them, "Y'all come on—you gotta hear this!"

We brought them to the house, where Dad told them about Jesus, and then we watched them all be baptized that night. The water was cold, and a few of them hollered at the shock, but I'll never forget it. I thought life could not possibly get better than it was that moment.

Jesus and His love and grace were what I thought about most during those months, and I had a lot of time on my hands to think.

Before long, something unexpected happened to test my new-found faith. Mom had to go in for a simple, twenty-minute surgery.

I went with Dad to the hospital, and we waited while she was in the operating room.

Forty-five minutes went by, and no one came out to tell us anything. Then a nurse came out, and one look at her face told me the news was not good.

"Look, there's a problem," she said. "We haven't been able to wake her up. She's gone into a coma. We have a machine breathing for her, and we think she's going to be okay, but she needs to wake up."

Dad looked at me, his face white and his eyes big and scared. We had no idea what was going on, but we knew it was bad. Really bad.

He grabbed my shoulder and said through tears, "We're fixin' to pray for your mom right now."

I'd never heard him pray as fervently. He was frantic and telling God about how much we needed Mom in our family. We knew her life was at stake, and we both were scared she would never wake up.

The rest of the family came to the hospital, and we gathered, praying our hearts out. We finally got in to see her, and the sight of Mom on a respirator, her chest rising and falling with the help of the machine, freaked us all out. Eventually, we found out what had happened. There had been a mistake, and Mom had been given too much anesthetic, sending her into a serious coma.

Two days later, after many tears and huddles with family and desperate prayers, Mom came out of it, woke up, and started breathing on her own. I knew deep in my heart that she could have died, but God had chosen to answer our prayers, and that really built my faith. I was such a new Christian that I'm not sure how I would have reacted if something would have happened to my mom. I also felt like it drew me closer to my dad, as we had been the first ones to hear the news and to pray for her together. I saw a side of him I didn't see very often, how much he loved and needed my mom and how much he trusted God to help him in a very bad situation.

No matter whose fault it was, we were just relieved Mom made it out alive. She recovered from the experience, and with her cooking during those months, my appetite came back, and I gained fifty pounds. I even got a little chunky, so I started working out so I could look and feel better. Those three months of house arrest were probably the best days of my life. My thinking had changed, my heart's desires were back on track, and I had hope for the future.

FOURTEEN

The Gap

Jep

Conscience is a man's compass.

—Vincent Van Gogh, letter to Theo

"IF YOU WANT TO CHANGE YOUR LIFE, YOU HAVE TO CHANGE YOUR friends," Mom always says. So while I was on the agreed-to house arrest, living down at the river with my parents and hunting every day, I stayed away from my hard-living friends in town. To stay busy, I worked and hunted, but best of all, I had so many good talks with Dad.

We'd be on our way to church, one of the few places I could go during those months, and he'd point at the church building when we'd arrive and say, "You know, this isn't what this is all about, Jep."

Really? I thought going to church is exactly what this is all about. I was under the impression that if you didn't go to church, you were doing something wrong.

"The Bible says believers met in homes, not buildings," he'd continue. "It's all about your heart, son, not the building. Look, the reason we go to church is for fellowship. To be with our brothers and sisters, meet with them, sing, pray, check on each other, all that great stuff."

It took me a while to wrap my mind around this idea—church was about getting to know God and getting right with God, and that it didn't have to happen in a church building. I finally began to understand when I realized that the act of going to church hadn't saved me from my bad choices before. My ritual of going to church services to please my parents and keep the peace in my family hadn't meant much because my heart hadn't been in it. I had been far more interested in parties and girls and cuttin' up than getting to know my Creator and Savior.

That all began to change as I studied the Bible with my dad, spent time talking to my mom, and let the Word of God begin the process of changing me. It didn't happen overnight, and there were stumbles along the way, but I worked hard to let go of the chase for the perfect high and, instead, started on the chase for a godly life.

I also realized I was blessed to have spent only six months in the pit of alcohol and drug abuse. My brother Alan had struggles that lasted a few years, and my dad was a prodigal for ten years. But I had the advantage of three brothers and two parents who saw me messing up my life and who stepped forward to pull me out of the pit. I understand now that the longer you stay in that kind of life, the worse you get and the harder it is to change. My dad had to lose just about everything, including his business, his wife, and his sons, before he turned to God. He was blessed in that my mom forgave him and let him come back. My brother lost much, too, and even came close to losing his life in a violent altercation when he was young.

I knew I was so blessed to experience a restart at such a young age because I'm not sure what would have happened if I'd continued on the road I was on. When I think back on some of those parties, I'm thankful there weren't hard drugs, such as heroin, because I probably would have tried it.

The months and years following my intervention I think of as my gap period, the time between the family intervention and meeting Jess. I stayed in my parents' house for a while then moved to a trailer next door, where I lived with my buddy Jason. After a few months, when Dad felt I could handle it, I moved in with Trey, who was living in his grandparents' house while his parents tried to sell it. It was a big, beautiful house with a swimming pool, and since they needed short-term renters, I paid something like $300 a month. My buddy Jason wasn't happy that I abandoned him in the trailer down by the river, but living with Trey was a deal I couldn't refuse.

I loved God and was learning how to follow Him, but I still didn't have it all together. One time I went on a road trip to Texas with a friend. He was seeing a girl there, and she invited us to a big summer get-together. We knew some of the people there and decided to go. We had a good time the first day, just hanging out. The next day, a few of us decided to head into town and visit a surf shop. As we browsed through the racks of board shorts, someone said, "You could take some of these shorts, and no one would know."

Really? I'd never thought about doing something like that. My dad had drilled into me and my brothers never to take anything that wasn't ours, and if we borrowed anything, we'd better take care of it and give it back in excellent condition. But it was tempting. I didn't have any money, and the day before I'd had to swim in my athletic shorts.

"I'll go talk to them up front, and you guys can do it," the guy said.

Without thinking anymore about it, we grabbed some board shorts, stuffed them down our pants, and walked out of the store. The guy up front walked out behind us, and I was kind of nervous.

"Man, I just don't feel good about that," I said in the car. I knew it was wrong, but we'd already done it, and what could I do now? I felt terrible and barely slept at all.

The next day we were riding around in the car when the cops pulled us over. We were freaking out, thinking we were about to get busted. As the police officer walked up to the side of the car, my friend said to us, "I got this. Don't say a word."

The officer asked if we'd been to the surf shop. "I have a description of you."

"No, we haven't been there," my friend said.

"Let me get a picture of each of you," said the officer.

That's it. We are going to jail, I thought. It was a desperate situation. What were we going to do? We couldn't run. We couldn't hide. And my dad was going to kill me when he found out.

We got out of the car, and he took our pictures. Then we had to tell him where we were staying, and after that he let us go. We drove straight home, and I ran in the house where we were staying, grabbed the board shorts, and took them outside. I dug a hole and buried them.

We grabbed our stuff and hightailed it back to Louisiana. We found out later the guy who'd gone with us and distracted the clerk at the front had returned to the store the next day and stolen a whole bunch of stuff, which is why the cops were looking for him. It was the one and only time I ever stole anything, and it was the worst feeling. I still feel bad about it.

But even though I still did some stupid things, my conscience was coming back online, and that was a good thing. I realized my conscience had been seared, almost as if it had gone to sleep, during those latter teen years when I was making bad choice after bad choice even though I knew what I was doing was wrong.

———————

I was now working more hours at Duck Commander, with Dad, Mom, and Jase. The business was still located at Mom and Dad's place, and I took it more seriously. I also reenrolled at ULM and took my studies more seriously too. I tried several different majors, but no matter what the major was, I took as many history classes as I possibly could with my favorite teacher, the famous Dr. Jones. He was hilarious, the coolest cat ever. He was old when I was there, and I heard he kept teaching college classes until he was eighty-three years old.

On the first day of class, Dr. Jones would bring a prosthetic leg packed full of Tootsie Roll candies and then throw them around the room. He was the kind of teacher who got up on his desk and waved his arms to make sure the class paid attention and got what he was trying to say. He was always telling stories, and one of my favorites was about backpacking across the globe, traveling through Europe, the Middle East, Southwest Asia, India, the Far East, and through the Panama Canal. He'd find work as a dishwasher in little diners and sometimes would get robbed of his paycheck. But my favorite Dr. Jones stunt was during the final exam. Four football players would carry a wooden coffin into the classroom, with Dr. Jones stretched out inside, looking very dead.

"Sorry," one of the football players would announce. "We have very bad news. Dr. Jones has died."

A hush would come over the room.

Then the guy continued, "But you're going to take the exam anyway."

Then *boom!* Up would raise the arm of Dr. Jones, clutching a stack of exams for us.

When Dr. Jones really did die, thousands of people attended his memorial service at the football stadium. I didn't hear about it in time, or I would've gone. He was one of the most amazing guys I have ever met.

Besides school and working at Duck Commander, I spent time with friends, including girls. I was even engaged for a while, although we weren't right for each other, and it eventually ended with hurt feelings on both sides.

But by far my favorite memories of the gap period are of spending time with my dad and studying the Bible with Trey. Since the truth of the gospel and the good news of Christ's forgiveness were so new and real to us, we were on fire for God and spent a lot of time just reading through the Bible and talking about what it said with friends and family. Eventually, this led to nightly Bible studies at the house. We'd invite guys and girls over to eat, play board games, cards, or dominoes, and swim. It was so much fun, and we'd laugh and have a great time; then at some point we'd get into some great spiritual discussions and turn it into a Bible study. Some people didn't care and weren't interested, but some really heard the gospel for the first time, and we'd end up baptizing them in the swimming pool.

Right about then, I drove into town for a haircut at Connie Sue's—yes, there was a time I frequented the hair salon—and ran into a beautiful girl named Jessica.

FIFTEEN

Jeep Headlights

Jess

And all who have been united with Christ in baptism
have put on Christ, like putting on new clothes.

—**Galatians 3:27** NLT

LONG BEFORE I EVER SAW HIM COMING INTO CONNIE SUE'S SALON, A
friend of mine in high school was always talking about a guy named
Jeptha. She was very sweet. She went to the Pentecostal church and
dressed very conservatively—hair down to her booty, skirts, little
makeup. We had history class together, and she used to let me put
mascara on her.

"He's a dream," she used to say. I could tell she had a crush on this
guy, and I'd just roll my eyes and shake my head.

I doubt it, I'd say to myself, after the thousandth time she'd talked
about Jeptha and called him dreamy again.

I was familiar with the name but not the actual guy, and it wasn't until the glide-by at Connie Sue's that I came face-to-face with the dream. *Whoops!* I mean, with Jeptha. I didn't think a whole lot more about him until I saw him again a couple of weeks later at a music club called Edge of Madness. There was no drinking, just music, and lots of kids hanging out.

The Jeptha came up to me during a break in the music and introduced himself.

"Hi. I'm Jeptha Robertson. Are you Jessica?"

Connie Sue had told him my name and a little bit about me, but I guess he wanted to make sure.

"Hi," I said, and smiled back.

"My dad is the Duck Commander," he offered.

Who? I didn't answer because I didn't know what to say. I had no idea who or what the Duck Commander was.

"You don't know who the Duck Commander is?"

I shook my head no. I'm sure I looked as confused as I felt. *Obviously, I am missing something, and I should know who the Duck Commander is.*

"You don't know who Phil Robertson is?"

No, again.

We chatted a little, and I could see he was trying to connect with me. Then he pulled out his best line: "Do you like my plaid pants?"

I looked at the familiar logo on his shirt and pants and thought to myself, *Wow, you must really like Abercrombie and Fitch.*

Surprised, I looked down and beheld his brown, green, and white plaid pants. You couldn't miss them. They definitely stood out in the crowd.

"Yeah," I said, my voice trailing off. I wasn't quite sure what else to say.

Now at least I know who the dream is, I thought. *And he is pretty cute.*

Then I saw some friends and wandered away. I went home and didn't think too much about him. I was still very raw emotionally from my failed marriage and from the bad choices I'd made in the three months after I'd left. I wasn't looking to get into a new relationship because I was still struggling to make sense of my own mistakes, my heartbreaks, my shame, and my doubts. To be honest, I never thought Jeptha could ever be interested in me.

I'd been shunned by so many after deciding to separate from my husband. When you live in the Bible Belt, you are frowned upon when a marriage ends. When you're married to a pastor, that feeling is multiplied by about a million. I felt like a failure since I'd only been married for a year and nothing had worked out like it should have. In my very deepest self, I felt something was wrong with me and I'd never get a second chance at love. I was a broken girl desperate for a bit of kindness. And I was just twenty years old.

The next time I saw Jep was a few weeks later at a chance meeting in a Chili's restaurant in town. He was there with friends, and I was there with family. We exchanged a few words, and then he and Trey invited me to their house to play games and do Bible study.

Something inside me woke up and told me to say yes, so I did. The night after Chili's I drove over to their house and joined a group of lively, fun-loving people who were as excited about God's Word as they were about playing spades and dominoes.

Jep was friendly and kind although he was quiet. Trey was very outspoken about his faith and excited about the gospel, so after a while he brought out his Bible and read some verses, explained what they meant, and led a discussion.

Although I'd been going to church with my mamaw, mom, and

sister my entire life, I had not been to Bible studies nor spent much time reading my Bible or talking about it with people. This was all new to me, and I wanted more. Coming from such a low place, emotionally and spiritually, I was looking for help and for hope. Something in those group conversations about Jesus spoke to me on a very deep level. My heart and soul were hungry and hurting, and I wanted to be fed.

Over the next few weeks, I became serious about attending church on Sundays and Wednesdays. On other nights of the week, I was often at Jep and Trey's house, hanging out with them and their friends, both guys and girls, and joining in the nightly Bible studies. I was beginning to understand that being a Christian wasn't just about going to a local church on Sundays with your family and trying to be good and not break the rules. Following God wasn't just about being a good girl and trying to keep everyone around me happy, which I'd obviously failed at. Instead, it was about a relationship with God, starting with understanding and accepting the sacrifice Jesus had made for me when He died on the cross for my sins.

My choices and lifestyle began to change. I stopped hanging around people who wanted to use me but didn't really care about me. Growing up, I'd felt safe and protected by my family, but once I was married, and it didn't work out, I felt embarrassed and ashamed and so far from God because I'd broken the rules.

I didn't remember ever hearing the gospel all of those Sundays in church. But now it seemed so simple. Jesus was God's Son, and He came to earth for us. For me. He knew me inside and out, He knew everything I'd ever done, and He came to earth to die and pay the price for my sins. One night I had a moment of clarity—I suddenly saw what I was really doing and how I was not really a Christian. I hadn't been following God with my whole heart. Instead, I'd walked the walk and played the part of a Christian, feeling like I could get to heaven with my good behavior. I finally understood that God had made a way for me to be forgiven of all of my bad choices through Jesus and His death on the cross. And when He rose from the grave on the third day, He conquered death forever. Somehow I had missed this simple story that changed everything for me and made sure I had a place in heaven. I wanted what the gospel promised.

I've never been slow to act, and one night at Jep and Trey's, when the light went on in my heart, and I really, finally understood, I immediately felt an urgency to act.

"I think I need to be baptized," I said suddenly, interrupting Trey.

I think my outburst surprised him and kind of stopped him in his tracks. It was dark outside, about eleven at night.

"Let's study some more," said Trey.

He kept going, reading some verses and explaining them.

"No," I interrupted. "I need to do it right now. I don't want to wait!"

There was a wanting inside of me to feel clean, to feel like a new person. I wanted to obey the gospel and be baptized right then, that night, in that very moment.

Trey gave in. "Okay, if that's what you want."

"Yes, right now!"

My heart began to glow with the thought. I felt hopeful and overcome with the love that I felt—that Jesus Christ would die for me so I could have the opportunity to live forever. Why would He do that? Even for just one sheep, one person to know, He would sacrifice Himself, even for me, just so I would have hope and His blood that covers all my sins. Of course I wanted to be baptized and start my life new.

Jep let me change into some old sweats of his, grabbed some towels, and the three of us hurried outside and piled into his green

Jeep CJ5. It had a soft top, and the only heat was from the engine. But it was April, and the air wasn't too cool yet, so it felt okay.

I was nervous and excited as we drove to a nearby lake. Man, I should've thought about snakes and alligators, but all I could think about was God and the incredible gift of a fresh start.

Jep pulled the Jeep up to the edge of the lake and pointed his headlights out over the water. We got out, and Trey waited in the grass on the side (maybe he was worried about the alligators too) while Jep and I waded out into the water until we were about waist deep. It felt cool and refreshing, and I was more awake than I had been in a very long time.

We stood facing each other, and Jep began.

"Do you believe that Jesus is the Christ, Son of the Living God, your Lord and your Savior?"

I shivered with excitement as I looked at Jep's face and hair, glowing in the headlights. "Yes."

Then he moved to my side, took my hand, and put his other hand gently on my back.

"Jessica, I now baptize you in the name of the Father, and of the Son, and of the Holy Spirit."

I let myself go and fell backward into the water, feeling safe in Jep's hands. I went all the way in, holding my breath with my eyes closed, and felt the cool water all around me. A split second later, Jep pulled me up into the night air as the water streamed off of me, and I rubbed my eyes and pushed back my long hair.

"You just made the best decision of your entire life," Jep said quietly, and gave me a quick hug. "You're my sister in Christ now."

I was filled with joy. I felt relieved and renewed, like a different person, as we sloshed our way through the lake and back to where Trey was waiting at the Jeep. He was excited and gave me a quick hug too. I grabbed a towel and dried off the best I could. I started to feel the chill then, but I was so excited it didn't seem to sink in.

We hopped back in the Jeep, and all the way back to the house, wrapped in the soggy towel, I talked to God in my heart. *I'm starting over, and I'm giving my life to you, Lord.* I felt so different. I didn't feel broken anymore or weighed down by the bad things that had happened over the last couple of years, many of them because of my own insecurities, weaknesses, and bad choices. It felt surreal to no longer have my past held against me. I was forgiven, and I felt new. It was the best day of my life.

SIXTEEN

Kissing Bandit

Jess

Kisses are the messengers of love and tenderness.

—Ingrid Bergman

AFTER JEP BAPTIZED ME, WE CONTINUED TO SEE EACH OTHER AT church and at Bible study, and our friendship grew. Besides being super cute, Jep is funny. He's quiet, but he has these looks, like a raised eyebrow, that made Trey and me laugh. I also noticed how sweet and kind he was to others. But I still didn't think he'd be interested in a girl like me.

He was definitely a little on the flirty side with other girls, and back in the ninth grade, he and his buddy Blake McGee called themselves "the kissing bandits" and competed to see how many girls they could kiss.

In June, a couple months after I was baptized, we all went on a group camping trip, and Jep and I rode down in the same car. We hung out together on the trip, and he was friendly and affectionate, holding my hand or putting his head in my lap. I think it was on this camping trip where our relationship started. We didn't say we liked each other—it was kind of like the unspoken obvious. But other people on the trip noticed. And people started to make comments after we got home. They noticed how we looked at each other, how we smiled, but maybe we were in just a little bit of denial. It reminds me of the country song about smiling a little too much, about how we stare just a little too long.

Jep and I weren't committed at this point, and still just mostly friends, but we had a moment at a bowling alley that seemed to signal a change in our relationship when he flirted with an old flame right in front of me.

I thought, *Okay. That's how it's going to be, hmm?* And I started talking to the boys we were bowling with, just visiting and having fun. And I could tell it bothered him.

"What's wrong? What are you doing?" he asked.

"Nothing. What do you mean?" I said, knowing exactly what he was talking about.

He wanted my full attention, but he still wanted to be able to talk to other girls. He didn't like me off visiting with other people and having a good time without him. Something changed, and after that night, we started spending more time together.

One day, when we were hanging out at his house, I started to think he might really like me. He stood up to give me a hug, and I could tell he wanted to kiss me, but I didn't want to make it too easy on him. *I'm not leanin' in*, I thought.

For some reason he was waiting for me to make the first move. He took forever, but he finally got the message, and he leaned in and gave me a kiss. It was the lightest kiss—very sweet. He's gentle and strong at the same time. And that was the end of the kissing bandit. He retired after that.

The more I got to know Jep, the more I realized we had a lot in common. We both had been raised around the table with big family dinners, hunting and fishing, and spending time with family. Jep loved his car, so for fun I'd put on camo, and we'd go riding around in his Jeep, splashing through mud holes and getting covered in mud. I also went with him to visit a struggling family in a very poor neighborhood. The family knew Jep very well, and it was clear they had a long-standing relationship with the Robertson family. Jep brought deer meat and ducks to share, stashed in an ice chest in the back of his Jeep.

I stayed in the car and watched while he carried the meat up a set of decrepit, broken-down stairs and into an older woman's house. But something unusual happened when he came out—he tripped on the way back down the stairs and started a spectacular flying leap that ended in a face-plant at the bottom of the stairs. He wasn't hurt, but I'll never forget the look on the old woman's face as she watched Jep's acrobatics.

"Well, look at you, boy," she said as he fell.

How could you not fall in love with a guy who would sacrifice his body to deliver food to the poor?

I also learned a lesson about the Robertson men when I went over to Jep's one night to play cards. Growing up, I never played board games or cards. I was just too busy running around outside, riding ATVs or practicing my gymnastics to slow down and play a game. But Jep loved games so I decided to try.

"Let's play rummy," he said.

"I don't know how to play," I said. "You'll have to teach me."

He gave me a rundown on the basics; then we started a game. For some strange reason I was able to beat him at rummy even though he'd been playing the card game his whole life. So we moved on to dominoes. Again Jep taught me the basics, and we practiced a little then started a game. I beat him again. He wasn't smiling and raising his eyebrow anymore, and I could tell the competition was heating up and he wasn't enjoying losing to me.

We moved on to board games, and he pulled out Battleship.

"I've never played it," I said.

"Okay, I'll teach you."

And wouldn't you know it? I won again. Although I wasn't as outwardly competitive as the Robertson clan, you have to have a strong competitive streak to do well in sports, and I definitely had that inside me. I liked winning, but I could tell Jep didn't like losing.

I found out later that the Robertsons were extremely competitive and played for blood, whether it was Monopoly, dominoes, or card games. But back then I didn't know, and what Jep said next really surprised me.

"I want you to leave." His face was stern and his eyes hard.

"What?" I said, laughing. I thought he was joking. He wasn't.

"I want you to leave this house right now."

"You want me to leave?"

"Yes."

So I did. I gathered up my stuff, walked out the front door, and got in my car. Jep trailed behind, and right before I drove away, he leaned over and said, "I'm sorry I'm so competitive. I learned it from my grandparents, my dad, and my uncles."

He told me later about the domino games at Granny and Pa's with loud arguing and slamming of dominoes on the table.

"I knew those games," Jep said. "I was really good. None of my friends could stay with me at all, so when you beat me, I was embarrassed. Nobody was supposed to beat me at those games."

So we learned early on to only play on the same team. We never play against each other if we can help it. Otherwise, I'll be out in the doghouse when I beat Jep!

We still hadn't really committed to an exclusive relationship yet and were free to date others, until one particular Sunday morning. I drove over to the house Jep shared with Trey. Jep let me in. I thought we'd go to church together, but he'd stayed up too late the night before and was planning to skip church that morning. We talked for a little while, and then I got up to go on to church alone.

"I don't want to you to leave," Jep said, surprising me.

"I'm gonna go," I said, ready to walk out the door.

"Don't leave," he said again. "I think I'm falling in love with you."

I didn't know what to say.

He gave me a hug and kiss. "I know I am," he added.

His tenderness and affection made me feel great. Even though I'd turned my life over to the Lord, I was still battling the familiar feelings of worthlessness. I was still damaged in so many ways and still healing. For him to say he loved me meant so much. After that, we committed to each other and spent even more time together. I was falling for him too.

As we got closer over the summer months, his friends, both girls and guys, began to express some concern over our relationship. It was a little awkward—I was still going through some issues with the divorce. At first, no one really said anything, and they were friendly to me and acted as though they wanted me around, but they didn't like us getting close.

Some of his buddies would come by to visit, and they began to ask me questions about my past. With a few of them it felt as if I was being drilled or interrogated, and it made me feel terrible about myself. This ugly voice started popping into my head, telling me, *Maybe you're not forgiven. Maybe you're just a terrible person.* Plus, a few of the girls at church, although they were just friends, were very protective and possessive of their Jeptha.

A bright spot, however, was meeting the Robertson family at church. The first one I was officially introduced to was Miss Kay.

"Mom, this is Jessica," Jep said.

Miss Kay came up and gave me a big bear hug, wrapping her arms around me. Jep was quiet while I soaked in her warmth and caring personality.

Her sweetness reminded me of my grandmother, who radiates love to everyone she meets. I felt a strong connection to her from the very first moment. We both loved Jep, and that was enough to start us off on a lifelong friendship, and she quickly became a true friend.

I also met Phil, and I gave him a big hug. It was a tiny bit awkward at first because he's not much of a hugger. But I didn't care. I loved him because he was Jep's dad.

I didn't see Willie and Jase and their families much, but Jep and Alan are really close, so we spent time as a couple with Alan and his wife, Lisa. There is such a big age gap between Alan and Jep that they are almost like father and son or uncle and nephew. Alan and Lisa were warm and caring and my past didn't seem to matter to them. I felt completely and totally comfortable with them.

I still felt pressure and disapproval, though, from Jep's friends, including some who were in a men's Bible study group with him. I was very confused because I didn't want to be the cause of any conflict in Jep's life. These were people he'd grown up with and admired, and I didn't want to pull him away from anyone or get in the middle of his relationships. I knew his men's group and his Christian friends were very important to him, helping him to make good choices and grow in his relationship with the Lord. But I was also beginning to feel that we were supposed to be together, so it was a confusing time. Even Trey, who'd been there when Jep baptized me, was worried.

"Man, she's got a lot to get over," he said to Jep. "She needs time to get her spiritual life together."

Jep told me about his broken engagement. He had given his fiancé a ring, and the breakup crushed him. He said it made it hard for him to trust women. He hadn't yet forgiven her and still had strong feelings of anger and betrayal. So even though we were falling in love, there were emotional struggles and scars from our pasts that were lurking beneath the surface of our relationship.

Eventually, his friends' concerns hit a tipping point, and Jep was forced to make a big choice.

SEVENTEEN

Blindsided

Jep

In a hundred lifetimes, in a hundred worlds, in any
version of reality, I'd find you and I'd choose you.

—Kiersten White, *The Chaos of Stars*

AS I GOT TO KNOW JESSICA MORE, I STARTED TO REALLY CARE FOR HER. Of every girl I've ever known, she reminds me most of my mom. But when we met, I also knew she was going through a divorce, and I wasn't sure if she was right for me. There was baggage involved, I'd already had my heart broken a couple of times, and I was scared. But I was falling for her, and as much as I tried, I couldn't force myself to ignore those feelings.

When my friends began to voice their doubts and concerns, it was even harder. None of my friends wanted us to be together. They said she wasn't good enough for me. I loved her, but I also wanted to keep my friends, and I felt torn.

I also had issues with trusting women after the broken engagement even though my feelings for Jessica were in a whole different league from my feelings for my ex-fiancée. Trey was there when that relationship had gone bad, and I think that's why he was down on Jessica.

"Man, we just need to wait," he told me. "We don't need to get married early. Let's go to college, get out, and get a good job before we go down that road."

He was a loyal friend and was trying to protect me from getting hurt again.

With everyone upset about my relationship with Jess, I had a hard time sorting out my feelings. I've always been the kind of person who takes awhile to process things, and I need time and space. I'm not the type to talk it out and then make a quick decision. But once I commit, I'm all in, just like I was with basketball and even way back in my Rocky Balboa days.

One night in the summertime I went to church and walked into a big surprise at my men's Bible study group. A church elder was in attendance. We always had the same group of guys so this was out of the ordinary. I sat down, wondering what was going on. It didn't take too long to find out.

We sat around in a circle, and the elder opened with a prayer. Then he looked directly at me with a stern look.

"Jep," he said, "we're all here for you tonight. We hear that you've been involved with a girl of ill repute."

The room was silent. All eyes were on me. Suddenly, I realized this was an intervention. And it was aimed at me. I'd already been through a drug intervention with my family, but this one felt different. I suddenly felt sick to my stomach.

Wait! This is about me . . . and Jessica? What is going on here? What happened to Bible study? My mind was racing, but I stayed quiet as he continued. I'd never felt so embarrassed.

"Are you dating this girl?" he asked.

"No, not exactly."

I didn't feel we were formally dating yet, more just getting to know each other, but I didn't want to open my mouth and try to explain everything to him.

"Have you had a sexual relationship with this woman?" he asked.

I said no, but admitted we'd kissed.

"Hmm," he said.

Then he began throwing Bible verse after Bible verse at me about adulterous women, divorce, and remarriage. Nobody else talked. Just him. He asked more questions, turning it into what felt an awful lot like an interrogation.

Then he began to pressure me to end the relationship with her.

"You're a Robertson. You can't go down that road," he said. "It's a mistake."

I didn't say anything. I didn't know what to say. *I'm just going to sit here and listen to him and then get up and leave.*

In my heart I felt because I was a Robertson—with my brother Alan a pastor, my other brothers involved in ministry, and my dad an outspoken member of the church—I was being held to a higher standard. I had so much respect for these men, and this elder, but I also felt confused, angry, and blindsided.

When it was finally over, I went out to my truck, got inside, and slammed my hands against the steering wheel. *I will never go back there again*, I said to myself. I felt like my brothers in Christ had just turned on me without warning and called in an elder to deliver a biblical beatdown.

I knew what had happened to Jessica with the youth pastor wasn't right. She'd been taken advantage of, and while she'd gone into a tail-spin and made some bad choices, she had given her life to Jesus, and He had given her a brand-new start. I'd seen it for myself that night in the pond, in the glow of my headlights when I'd had the privilege of baptizing her into the kingdom of God.

What had just happened was so different from the family meeting that had rescued me from the addiction pit. This time, the intervention felt unfair, self-righteous, and judgmental, and it just didn't sit right with me. To be honest, it had the opposite effect and drove me more toward Jessica than away.

When I got home, I called Jess and told her what had happened. It was hard for her, too, because she didn't want to be the cause of all this.

"We can always go to a different church," I said.

The meeting, and my anger and confusion, caused a split between me and my Bible study friends. I didn't know what to do. *Could the elder be right? Is it wrong to be falling in love with Jessica?* It didn't feel wrong. But I'd learned to trust God's Word; and before I got more serious with this girl, I needed to know exactly what it said about divorce and remarriage, so I turned to my dad. I knew he would tell me the truth.

First, he read verses from Luke 7, about the woman who anointed Jesus. The Bible says she was a sinful woman—probably an adulteress or even a prostitute. But Jesus saw her heart, and He forgave her and gave her a brand-new start.

"I tell you, her many sins have been forgiven—as her great love has shown. But whoever has been forgiven little loves little," said Jesus, talking to the people around them. Then Jesus said to her directly, "Your sins are forgiven."

The other people said, "Who is this who even forgives sins?" They were questioning Jesus' actions and His authority.

"Your faith has saved you; go in peace," Jesus said to her (Luke 7:47–50 NIV). At that moment, He didn't care what the others thought or what they were saying. He saw a broken woman, and He gave her a new life.

I'll never forget what Dad said next.

"Jessica has a lot of baggage. That road is going to be a little bit harder for you."

I knew he was right.

"But since she is a child of God Almighty, she is forgiven," he continued. "If you love her, and you can't be without her, then that is the road you should take. She is forgiven, and her sins have been washed clean by the blood of Christ."

"I know," I said. "I knew that. But when you hear all of that other stuff, it's confusing."

"You got no problem with the Lord, son," Dad said.

My dad had struggled and been forgiven too. He knew what it was like to be judged and looked down upon for his past. Later on in another conversation, we talked more about forgiveness.

"Son, you'll want your kids to have as sinless a life as possible. But it's not possible to be perfect although some people, like your brother Jase, have lived a less sinful life than others."

Jase is a strong man. But Dad and I are different from Jase and from others who somehow are able to stay on the straight and narrow just about all the time.

"Those people will never understand forgiveness as you and I will," said Dad. "You and I could have died. People who've done something like that really understand forgiveness."

I also talked to my mom and told her what had happened. She loved Jess and knew she was a good person. I told my mom that Jess was so much like her, and that made her happy. When I left Mom and Dad's house that night, the stress was gone, lifted away by Bible verses we'd read together.

A week later I was at church, and I saw an elder, a different one. He'd heard what had happened at the meeting, and he came up to me and put his arm around me. I wasn't expecting him to say anything, and I was really surprised when he told me this: "Son, some people around here are idiots. That girl is right by God. If you love her, son, get married, start a family, and name one of 'em after me."

In the end, I didn't blame the elder or my friends for anything they said or did. They were trying to watch out for me and didn't want to lose me. It's just that they were wrong. Jessica was forgiven. And I also knew what it was to be forgiven. I'd been through my own share of struggles and understood what it meant to feel the love and mercy of God. I knew in my heart that I was to show that same forgiveness to Jessica.

She was still worried, though.

"I don't want you to choose me over your friends," she said one day at my house. "I don't want them to hate me even more."

"What they're saying isn't right. I know it's not right. And they'll get over it."

I was starting to realize how deep my feelings were for her, and I wanted to let her know.

"I love who I am when I'm with you. We took the long way around, but we were destined to be together. I love you."

"I love you too," she said.

"We'll just go to a different church if we have to. Don't worry about my friends."

She smiled.

"I choose you," I said and reached out my arms to her.

EIGHTEEN

The Beach-House Letter

Jess

Honesty is the first chapter of the book of wisdom.

—Thomas Jefferson

AFTER THE MEN'S GROUP TRIED THEIR BEST TO BREAK US UP, WE BEGAN to grow closer, and our relationship started moving more quickly. Jep pulled away from his friends a bit, and the rest of the summer we saw each other every day. We hung out, went to movies, started spending time with both our families, and began doing Bible studies together.

This time everything felt different. Instead of feeling pressured by everyone around me to be with a man even though it felt wrong, I felt pressured not to be with this man even though it felt right. I was learning we'd have to fight to be together, and it would have been much easier to cave-in to the pressures and strains that were pulling us apart, starting from that very first moment at Connie Sue's.

The odds were always against us. But I loved my Jules, and he loved me. Our bond was growing deeper. I think it helped that we started as friends, got to know each other without the immediate pressures of dating, and grew close emotionally and spiritually before we took our relationship to a more serious level.

That summer we also went on a couple of beach vacations together. My parents invited Jep on a family trip to Destin, Florida, and we had a great, relaxing time. Then it was my turn to join his family when I was invited on the annual Robertson family beach vacation for Labor Day weekend. Everyone goes, except Phil and Uncle Si, and everybody stays in one big house with ten or twelve bedrooms, two living rooms, and two kitchens. The rooms are full of noise, laughter, sand everywhere, and the smell of Miss Kay's homemade biscuits. The family cooks together every night, taking turns making their specialties and trying to outdo each other. Willie usually wins.

I was excited to spend time with the family, including the cute little Robertsons—John Luke, Sadie, Reed, and Cole. Every day the brothers woke up early and went out to play at least one round of golf. The girls stayed behind to lay out in the sun, hang out with the kids, read books, eat a chicken salad lunch, and shop at the outlets. In the afternoons and evenings, when we weren't on the beach, we'd play board games or just sit on the patio and enjoy the fresh ocean air.

At first, I was a little nervous, but it was always easy for me to chat, and the girls made me feel comfortable, especially when we were cooking or cleaning up together.

Whenever he wasn't playing golf and whenever I could get away, Jep and I spent time together. In Florida we had started talking about the future. *Our* future.

We both knew we weren't dating just to date. We talked about marriage and what we wanted in a mate. We talked about how many kids we wanted—we both wanted four! And I agreed when Jep said he wanted me to be able to stay at home with the kids.

"That's what I want to do," I said. My dream of being a wife and mother seemed possible again, when just earlier that year it had seemed like a dream that had been torn apart, crushed down, and just about destroyed. But after I studied God's Word with Jep, and we later started dating, everything happened so quickly I almost wanted to hold my breath and wait for something to go wrong because it seemed too good to be true.

And, of course, it was because the closer we got, and especially as we began to think about and plan for the future, my old insecurities began to rise to the surface. *Am I good enough for him? Am I good enough for the Robertson family? Can I make it work this time? Will I be a good wife?*

Suddenly, about halfway through the trip, I began to feel overwhelmed as I thought about my first marriage and my bad choices during the separation. I had started living a lifestyle I never thought I'd live and had tried to cover up my brokenness with attention from other men. I hadn't told Jep everything yet, and that day at the beach house, while he was out golfing, I began to feel the heavy burden of that three-month period in my life. Sometimes people say "your past is your past, and you can't change it," and that is true; but when you love someone and plan to spend the rest of your life with him, I think it's important to come clean and be honest. Even though I had already confessed everything to God and asked for His forgiveness, my past mistakes were still a burden, like a rotten, festering weight on my chest, and I needed to get free before I could move forward with Jep. I had screwed up badly, and I didn't want to seem to be someone I wasn't. I wanted to come clean. I didn't want to live a lie.

I knew telling him everything would be a risk, and I agonized over it. *What if he thinks I'm a horrible person? What if he breaks up with me? What if . . . he hates me?* But in the end, it didn't matter. I knew I had to tell him. Somehow I couldn't tell him out loud, so I wrote a letter. It was several pages long, and I remember sitting in my room with the sun streaming in through the windows and my tears falling on the pages as I poured out my heart to my love.

I wrote all day long while Jep was gone. I didn't name names, but I told him everything I had ever done. Deep down, I truly felt that once he read the letter, he would never love me again. But still I had to do it.

I finished the letter, folded it up, and put it in my pocket. It felt heavy, both in my pocket and in my heart. Then I joined the others, greeting Jep when he got back from golf, and wondered, *Is this the last time you'll ever smile at me? Is this my last kiss?*

The afternoon, family dinner, and games crawled by, and I tried to hide my pain and my worry. Every once in a while I put my hand in my pocket, touched the letter, and prayed that Jep would understand. The folded-up sheets of paper were weightless, but the letter felt like a concrete block in my pocket; I couldn't ignore it or forget it, not even for a second.

Finally, the family got tired and, little by little, headed off to their rooms. Jep and I sat on the couch, cuddled, and talked late into the night until everyone else was in bed asleep. Then I knew it was time. My hand shook, and I felt icy cold as I pulled out the pages, handed them over, and said, "I have something I want you to read."

Then I sat. And I waited.

Jep looked at me with eyebrows raised, then unfolded the pages and started reading. I felt like I couldn't breathe. I watched his face, but he didn't show any expression at all, and I had no idea what was going to happen. I looked away and tried to stay calm, but I couldn't keep my eyes off him. He kept reading, his face beginning to take on a more serious, almost frozen look. Finally, he finished. Then he spoke.

"I don't know what to say."

"I had to get this off my chest," I said. "I had to tell you everything."

The tears started to well up in my eyes. My heart was on fire.

"I feel sick," he said, his face a mask.

He stood up, gripping the letter. "I need some time."

As he walked away, folding up the pages, I heard him say, "I think we need some time apart. We'll see what happens."

I had no more words. I had used them all up. The tears began to stream down my face, and I hurried to my room. This was it. What I had feared most was happening. Jep now knew everything I'd ever done, and he was going to be done with me. I crumpled down onto my bed, grabbed the covers, buried my face inside, and cried myself to sleep.

The next day was awful. Jep wasn't mean, but he was cold. My written confession had overwhelmed him and shut him down, and he spent the rest of the trip hanging out with his brothers. It was so awkward. I didn't know what to do. How could I stay there with his family when he wasn't talking to me? Everyone could tell something had happened.

I called my mom, as I did every day.

"Are you okay?" she asked. She could hear something in my voice.

"Well, Jep and I just broke up. I told him everything, all about how I messed up."

"Do you want me to come and get you? I'll drive there and pick you up and bring you home," she said.

I felt all alone, and I was tempted to take her up on her offer, but something inside of me said to stay. I cried a little and told her I'd be okay since it was just a few more days.

When I got off the phone, I wandered into the living room and found Miss Kay. She could tell I was upset, and within a few minutes I'd told her everything that happened.

"It's okay," she comforted me, so sweet and kind and loving. "That's all in your past now."

I also told Lisa, Alan's wife, and she was just as sweet to me. They were both loving and forgiving, and I started to feel just a tiny bit better. By their actions and their attitudes, I felt they were showing Jesus to me.

Even so, I still felt sad, alone, very awkward, and out of place. Miss Kay and Lisa, as kind as they were, were busy and had things to do, so it's not like they were holding my hand the whole time. I was already missing Jep, not having him there always beside me. I felt something was missing, as though I'd lost my closest friend and ally. I wasn't sure if I would ever have him back beside me again.

Toward the end of the week, it was family picture day, when everyone wore matching clothes and took portraits on the beach. The photographer took photos of each of the brothers and their families. It seemed strange, but he also took some shots of Jep and me together. We wore matching blue jeans and white T-shirts. We stood close together, but Jep's arms were pretty much hanging straight down. I rested my hand very lightly on the front of his shirt and tried to smile. Then it was time for the big family portrait. Of course I wasn't included, because I wasn't family, and I felt very awkward again. I didn't really belong, and I wasn't sure I ever would.

Jep and I did exchange a few words here and there. It was clear that he needed time to think about everything I'd told him and figure out his feelings. His words were few, but I was happy for each one. He seemed angry, but I could tell he was also trying to be nice. He said he still wanted to be friends but the warmth and feeling of connection we had was gone, and he wouldn't look into my eyes anymore. I missed holding his hand or touching his arm. I tried to be tough and strong, but I knew it was over. Even though I didn't think he loved me anymore, I still loved him. I realized I'd truly fallen for him. And there was also a tiny part of me that felt happy that I had opened up and shared everything with him.

My first marriage had not been an honest, open relationship. We hadn't been equals from the start, and I'd felt pressured and manipulated. But part of the problem was the secrecy. I'd kept our relationship secret for a whole year until I was eighteen, and I didn't feel I could tell anyone my true feelings.

This time was different. Jep knew everything, God knew everything, and I'd also shared everything with my mom and my sister, and with Miss Kay and Lisa. I was no longer isolated and broken down. Although I was devastated at the breakup, I had love and support from the wonderful people God had put around me. Through their support, I realized I had become a Christian not because of Jeptha but because I'd wanted to be a child of God. I would never go back to my old ways. I had a new family—my church family—my forever family.

Finally, beach week was over, and we headed home. Jep and I rode together in the backseat, and when he got tired, he put his head in my lap. It was confusing, but I wondered, *Is there still hope?*

NINETEEN

A Random Impulse

Jep

True love stories never have endings.

—**Richard Bach,** *The Bridge Across Forever*

I DON'T REMEMBER MUCH ABOUT THE BEACH HOUSE THAT SUMMER, except I was pumped to have Jessica join us. Our annual beach trips were always EBP, Everybody But Phil, and so it was cool to have my whole family together. I knew the more time they spent with Jessica, the more they would love her as I did.

At first, I had a great time, and I looked forward to seeing Jessica when I got home from golfing with my brothers. I especially looked forward to our late-night talks. I felt happy and comfortable around her, and whenever I was away from her, I couldn't wait to see her again.

But that night when she handed me the letter, I felt blindsided. I knew about her marriage and divorce, but I didn't know she'd been caught up in some bad stuff with other men. I didn't know what to think when I first read it. My stomach started hurting bad, and my very first thought was, *I need to take a break here.* I didn't say much, just walked away and went to my room to process through what she'd written. I don't remember what I did with the letter, probably threw it away or burned it. I knew I didn't want to read it ever again.

I remember thinking, *I wish she would've told me all this before we started dating. I could have given her more time.* I didn't want to pressure her or rush her into anything. I thought about what my buddies had said, especially Trey, about not rushing into anything. *Were they right?*

Her letter also explained why she'd been so anxious to be baptized that night at the pond. She'd been in a very dark place and didn't have a family intervention like I'd experienced. So when the chance came for forgiveness, and she understood the message of the gospel for the first time, she didn't want to wait even one more second.

While I was thinking about all of this, I didn't want to talk to her. I needed space, and I just hung around my brothers for the rest of the trip. It was awkward, and my stomach hurt. I hated the way it was, but that's just the way it was.

On the way home in the back of the Suburban, I grabbed her hand and held it. I couldn't help myself. I wanted to show her, even though I was hurt and confused, that I still cared about her. I didn't want her to think I didn't care. I got sleepy later and put my head in her lap. It felt right.

When we got home, we went our separate ways. That next week I went over and talked to my brother Alan. I also talked to my mom.

"You went through a lot of stuff before you became a Christian," she reminded me. I listened to Mom, and I knew it was true. I also knew there were a few things I'd done that I hadn't shared with Jessica, yet.

During the next week and a half, I thought about Jessica and the letter and tried to make sense of my feelings. I couldn't just ignore what she'd done, and part of me thought she might not be ready for marriage or even a serious relationship. She was a new believer and didn't have a strong spiritual foundation yet. She had a past and was still healing from all that had happened. And she was still only twenty years old.

But I couldn't stop thinking about Jess either. I wasn't over her, and I knew I wouldn't ever be over her. I still loved her. I just needed to be sure. I needed that time to think about everything and make sure. I wanted to pray about it, pray with others, and get some good advice. That was my deal. I wanted to make sure it was right, and everyone I talked to gave me positive feedback. The consensus was, "if her past is what's holding you back, and she's forgiven, then you're looking at this from the totally wrong angle." I'd had my own struggles, although mine were different, so who was I to hold her to a higher standard?

I sat beside Jess in a Wednesday night Bible study class at church. She held her head up and didn't say much. After class was over, I went up to her, and said, "Hey." I was trying to be cool. She said *hey* back; then I told her I missed her. I don't remember if I hugged her or not, but I know I wanted to.

"I miss you too," she said. And that's all it took. We started talking a little, and talking to our friends who talked to each other or to my mom. And within a few days we were hanging out again, spending time together.

One day soon after, we were sitting on the floor of my room together, reading the Bible. At that time I was living back at Mom and Dad's house. Jess and I were reading out loud through the New Testament. I was excited about reading it through and getting context because usually people just tend to pick out and read verses that they like. This way, I felt I was reading a story that was all coming together and making sense. As I was reading, I started thinking about Jessica and the idea of getting married. *We could be doing this—reading our Bibles, cooking our own food, hanging out—at our own house.* Suddenly, I was excited about the idea of leaving Mom and Dad's house and starting my own family with Jessica.

All my brothers had gotten married before they were twenty, and here I was twenty-two, and not married. I knew Jess was the one. *I'm not going to look at any more girls*, I thought, still reading through Scripture out loud. *I just want to get married to the woman I love.* There was a deep sense of knowing inside of me. I didn't want to overthink it anymore; I just wanted to do it. If we knew we wanted to be married, why wait? So all of a sudden I just burst out, "We should get married."

Jessica looked up from her Bible, surprised. I wasn't down on my knees, and I didn't have champagne or a ring, so she wasn't exactly expecting a marriage proposal. But that's what it was. A random impulse of a marriage proposal.

I looked in her eyes and said it again. "Let's get married. I want to spend the rest of my life with you."

There were hugs and tears, and then we ran out to tell Mom and Dad the news. More hugs, more tears. And wedding plans started right away.

"We'll just elope," I said, "or get Dad to marry us."

We didn't want to waste a second. Now that we knew, we wanted to get married as soon as possible and start our lives together. But Mom had a fit.

"No," she said in a loud voice. "We *have to* have a wedding. I've always dreamed about your wedding, Jep."

I didn't want a big wedding, and I knew it would take time and cost a lot of money.

"Mom, I just think it would be better this way."

"Look, just some family," she argued back, "and maybe some of my best friends. I'll help get everything together. It won't be hard. You'll see."

Then she tilted her head and smiled that big smile; how could I say no?

We finally gave in because we could see how important it was for her, but we made it clear we wanted to get married as soon as possible, so we set a date for two weeks away. We don't waste much time down here in Louisiana.

Although I'd been engaged once before, I felt I made the decision with a clear head this time. I'd taken some time to think things through and make sure I was getting married for the right reason. Jessica was beautiful and sweet and kind and caring. She loved me, but even more important, she loved God. And of all the girls I'd ever met, she still reminded me the most of my mom.

I didn't feel swept up in emotion. I felt she was right for me, and I was right for her. We were good together. We made each other better people. We still do.

We had only two weeks until the wedding, but we still managed to fit in some premarital counseling with Dad's best friend. Alan and Lisa met with us too; they were our go-to people for any questions or problems. We had some plans for the future but not in detail. I didn't worry too much about how we were going to make it financially or what the next few years would hold—I just wanted to start our lives together. I wanted to work, go hunting, have friends over once in a while, and most of all, come home to Jessica.

Mom generously cosigned for a three-bedroom trailer house for us to live in, and Jase and Missy agreed to let us put it in their backyard, so we had a place to live. Our payment was $250 a month.

Even though I was excited, I didn't tell any of my friends that I was about to get married. I kept to my normal routine, going to work, going to the gym, and hanging out with some of my buddies. And I never said a word. We didn't want to make a big deal about getting married, and we didn't want a huge fancy wedding.

Mom made all the arrangements and called in favors from her friends and people at church. The ceremony was planned for the backyard of Dad's best friend's house, and we didn't send out any wedding invitations. It was all word of mouth, and we invited only immediate family, not even all of the cousins. Jessica wore a pretty blue skirt and top from the sale rack at Dillard's. I borrowed slacks, along with a shirt, tie, and shoes from Alan.

I had no second thoughts and felt only excitement on our wedding day. I just couldn't believe it. *This is crazy! I'm actually getting married.* Somehow I'd thought I would be an eighteen-year-old forever, and I still liked being silly. But when Alan started the vows, I listened carefully because I wanted to really mean them. And I did mean it when I pledged to give my life to my wife. Divorce was not going to be an option.

We didn't have money for a fancy wedding or reception or even a honeymoon. Instead, we splurged on a big pasta dinner at the Olive Garden in town. That was our honeymoon, and it was the best night of my life.

TWENTY

The Puzzle

Jess

Marriage is getting to have a sleepover with your
best friend, every single night of the week.

—Christie Cook

WRITING THAT LETTER AND TELLING JEP EVERYTHING WAS SO HARD,
but in the end, it was a good thing. At first, Jep's shock and surprise
frightened me even though I expected it. *He'll never love me*, I thought.
He'll always think of what I did and the bad choices I've made. I beat myself
up every day, every hour, every minute even though I knew I was
forgiven.

But when Jep and I saw each other at church that next week, and
then he proposed shortly after, I was so glad I had confided in him and
shared my past. It was a quick turnaround—just two weeks later we'd
be getting married. There wasn't even time for Jep to ask my dad—I

just told my parents myself. They were a little hesitant, but they liked Jep a lot. My mom thought he was funny and sweet, and they saw how happy we were together.

We didn't spread the news around about the upcoming wedding. Since it was just immediate family, we didn't even send out invitations or put an announcement in the paper. Many people heard we'd broken up, and then before they knew it, we were married. A rumor floated around that I was pregnant, and that's why we were getting married, but it wasn't true. Both Jep and I, once we make a decision, like to move forward, and that's what we did. I loved Jep, I wanted to get married this time, and I was committed to staying with him through good times and bad.

During those two weeks before the wedding, Jep was busy working at Duck Commander, I was still working at a new nanny job, and we were going to premarital counseling. Meanwhile, Miss Kay was rounding up friends to help with the wedding. Our wedding and reception cost just a few hundred dollars. Some people put so much money, time, and effort into a wedding, but I wanted our wedding to be simple, small, and intimate. We'd wanted to elope and have Phil marry us, but Miss Kay put her foot down.

"We have to have a wedding and have family there. Let me put something together," she offered.

She ended up planning the whole thing in two weeks. I'm kind of a tomboy with this kind of thing even though I do like to dress up. There's so much pressure behind planning a wedding. I've seen women get so angry, but I have no patience for it, and a huge, elaborate wedding just isn't my style.

Jep felt the same. He didn't seem to care about the details at all. To him it was a hassle and more money he didn't want to spend. We just wanted to be married and start our lives together.

We got married on a Sunday, after going to church that morning. Right after church, Jep said, "I've got something to go do. I'll see you at two o'clock." Then he headed off to Zale's and spent his savings on a wedding band for me.

It was such a sweet occasion. Our families surrounded us, no more than a couple dozen people, including little Reed, Cole, John Luke, and Sadie. Alan performed the ceremony using quick, traditional vows. Missy sang, her beautiful voice such a blessing. Miss Kay's friend Grace made our simple, white wedding cake, and I'm not even sure what food was offered although I'm sure there were snacks and punch. Someone did flowers too. What I remember most is family around us, with Jep and me at the center, pledging to love each other for the rest of our lives.

This time I meant it. I didn't want to run away, I had no secrets from Jep, and I was about to marry the man who had baptized me into the kingdom of God. It was an awesome experience. I felt no pressure, only trust, joy, and optimism for the future and for our new lives together. Everything that had been taken away from me, or that I had thrown away through bad decisions, was being restored, and more.

After we said our vows and spent some time with the family, we slipped away to our new trailer house, about a quarter mile up the road. Jep and I couldn't afford a honeymoon, and that was fine with us, so after we changed our clothes and opened wedding gifts, we headed into town. Then we ate our wedding-night meal, just the two of us, at the Olive Garden. I'm sure Jep ordered the Tour of Italy platter, his favorite, with chicken parmesan, lasagna, and fettuccine Alfredo. I probably ordered the minestrone soup and salad. On a whim, we stopped at a store and bought a two-thousand-piece jigsaw puzzle with a Christmas theme. Jep was off work for a week, and we thought it would be fun to work on it together.

Our trailer honeymoon week was a dream. We spent all our time together in our new little house and worked on our puzzle, laughing and talking along the way. I just loved being with Jep. By the end of the week, we had finished putting the puzzle together, and later I found a big wooden picture frame for three dollars at Goodwill, glued the finished puzzle onto some backing cardboard, and framed it as a memory of our honeymoon. For seven or eight years I would get it out every year at Christmastime and hang it on the wall until finally one year it got wet and started to wrinkle. I had to throw it away, and Jep and I are still sad about the loss.

In the first few weeks of being married, when I wasn't down at Duck Commander with Jep, helping Miss Kay answer the phone or take orders, I worked on decorating the house by going to garage sales. I'd grown up going garage sale-ing with my mom and grandmother in Arcadia, and I loved anything old. I was always looking for old books, pictures, fabrics or tapestries, and antique furniture I could refinish. I'd call my decorating style vintage and eclectic. I also loved old tea cups and antique dishes. Miss Kay went with me to garage sales and antique stores to pick out a table, chairs, dressers, and a hutch. I began to feel like we were kindred spirits.

When Jep and I began to surface and see friends again at church or around town, we realized some of them were angry that we hadn't invited them or even told them we were getting married. But it all happened so fast. Eventually, they seemed to understand. We spent a lot of time with Jep's family, especially Alan and Lisa.

Miss Kay became like a best friend because I had cut ties with many of my friends from before I met Jep. I went to Bible studies with my mother-in-law at least once or twice a week, and I knew she would help me whether I had a question, a problem, or needed help to get Jep straightened out. She was wise in the ways of the Lord, and I listened and tried the best I could to do what she said. I felt comforted and connected when I was with her.

After we were married, Jep turned me into a night person. In high school, I'd been such an early bird, but Jep liked to stay up until about two in the morning, so I stayed up with him. He'd get up about nine in the morning for work—he could do his job any time of the day. Sometimes I'd go to bed earlier, but I wanted to spend time with him, so I adjusted my schedule.

When I wasn't working at my nanny job, I went down to Phil and Kay's to help, and sometimes I got to help Miss Kay make dinner. That's how I learned to make Jep's favorite dishes. One of his favorites was homemade spaghetti (I always put my own little twist on family recipes). I learned how Miss Kay browns the meat, adds the tomatoes and vegetables and spices, and then cooks the sauce in a Dutch oven for three hours. Miss Kay later bought crates and crates of my mamaw's garden tomatoes, and she trained me in canning tomatoes.

I also learned how to make Miss Kay's biscuits. I loved cooking big breakfasts for Jep, usually bacon, sausage, eggs, and biscuits. We were the first ones out of our group of church friends to get married, so his friends came for breakfast or dinner whenever they could. "I can't believe she makes all of this food," they'd say. I got lots of fresh vegetables from my grandparents, along with fresh bacon and ham from their hogs.

For dinner I either cooked or we ate with family. We hosted Bible studies, and several nights a week had friends over to play spades or dominoes. I loved going deer hunting with Jep. I'd help him put corn out in the feeders and sit with him in the deer blinds. I also went with him to take deer and duck meat to the houses of some of the older ladies at church. I loved how he treated them—sweet, gentle, and kind, not like most guys at that age.

A few months after we got married, we drove to Colorado with friends to enjoy the snow. Jep was a really good skier. I hadn't been skiing in several years, so I wasn't as good, but I loved the mountains and sitting around a cozy fireplace in the ski lodge.

About a month later we went to Las Vegas for Shot Show, a huge hunting, shooting, and outdoors trade show and conference. Duck Commander was there to display its wares and take orders, with the whole family going along to help. Jep and I went, along with Jase and Missy. Willie wasn't working at Duck Commander full time yet, but he usually came to the show to help out too. Phil and Miss Kay were there, and so was Uncle Si.

My first experience at Shot Show was a little unexpected, however. I was excited because I was anticipating some time with Jep in a lively city on a vacation we really couldn't afford on our own. I knew he'd be working the show, but I hoped we'd have some time to explore the city and spend time together. But for some reason we newlyweds were expected to share a room with Jase and Missy. It was a little on the awkward side. Here I was, new to the Robertson family, not very familiar with his older brother and his wife, and we all were sleeping on double beds in the same hotel room, just feet apart. And I don't mean for just one night. Shot Show lasted about five nights.

We did get out and walk around on the Strip. Jep, Miss Kay, and I posed for a picture with one of those big, painted pictures with face cutouts—Jep was Elvis in the middle, and Miss Kay and I were the showgirls in bikinis with tropical fruit hats.

We also splurged and went to see *Phantom of the Opera*. It was my first time going to a Broadway-style musical, and I loved it. I could relate to struggling to find true love. We did a little bit of gambling and card playing, and I remember visiting a Wild West town, right outside the city.

Mostly, though, Jep and I were kind of boring our first year of marriage. All we wanted to do was stay home and spend time together.

TWENTY-ONE

I'm Going to My Mom's

Jep

All marriages are happy. It's the living together
afterward that causes all the trouble.

—Raymond Hull

PEOPLE ALWAYS ASK ME WHAT IT'S LIKE TO WORK WITH MY FAMILY. I can't ever remember a time I didn't work with my family, whether it was duck calls or fishing or collecting Granny's money out of the box down by the dock. As a kid, when I was old enough, I worked on and off for Duck Commander, which was still located on my parents' property right next to the house.

Duck Commander always needed help, and I've done almost everything, including answering phones, packaging, shipping, making sales calls, staining and dipping the wooden duck calls, and carving reeds. The only thing I never really did, because Dad was so weird about it back then, was to operate the machine that turned and shaped the duck calls. Jase eventually trained enough with Dad that he was allowed to do it.

I really did enjoy working with my family and still do. Dad was the driving force behind everything. He was passionate about making and demonstrating the world's best duck call, and he instilled that passion in each of us. Working at Duck Commander was more than just a job that paid the bills—we were on a mission. He made us try out every duck call we made to make sure they worked right and sounded like the duck they were supposed to sound like.

Mom did the paperwork, kept the books, took orders, and provided customer service. She also cooked a homemade lunch, like meatloaf or her famous mac and cheese, for the entire workforce every single day. No bologna sandwiches for us!

Of my brothers, Jase has worked the longest at Duck Commander. Willie took a long break and went to college, and so did Alan, being a full-time minister, but both are back now. Working with my parents and my brothers has kept us close and communicating. If we didn't work together, I'd probably never see Jase because he'd always be out on the water somewhere catching something, and I'd never see Willie because his intensity and restless energy would keep him out on the road doing business deals and networking.

I really liked shipping, maybe because I got to use a computer. I thought that was cool. Or maybe I just enjoyed trying to stay organized and get the orders right. It was kind of busy work but fun work. Many of our orders went out to smaller stores or to individuals across the country. I loved thinking about how our duck calls were shipping into every state, and when I was younger, I loved going around with Mom and Dad on sales calls or to work the shows. One of the reasons

I think I'm so close to Dad is that time spent together traveling with him. Sometimes when he walks by, he slaps me on the butt, and he doesn't do that to anyone else. I take it as a sign of affection.

When hunting season came around, though, Dad's priority shifted from making duck calls to going out to hunt every single day. I joined him when I could or hunted with my brothers or my buddies. Jessica had gone hunting some with her dad. I'd been out with her dad a couple of times, and he had a beautiful deer stand with a heater. It was elegant and finished well and looked like a carpenter had built it. Dad's old deer stand wasn't near as nice. He'd built it twenty feet up in a big tree with a fork in the middle, and it was a ramshackle structure that I don't think had a level spot in it. There was a big, rickety old ladder attached. When Jessica came deer hunting with me, I had to talk her into climbing the ladder.

"Is this safe?"

"Oh, yeah," I reassured her.

She spotted some old rotten felt that Dad had used to insulate the blind; it had seen better times. She examined the mold and fungus covering the felt and asked, "What all is on that thing?"

"Oh, it's nothing," I said. "Don't worry about that."

Then she saw the spiders and started yelping.

"Ssshhh," I whispered. "We're deer hunting."

She tried to be quiet; I'll give her credit. But the spiders sent her over the edge.

"I can't handle it," she whispered back.

"Go on back to the truck. I won't be long," I said, helping her get back down the ladder.

Another time she went along with me to hunt snakes. We try to shoot as many cottonmouths on the property as possible, and I was walking away from the four-wheeler when I heard Jess say, "There's a snake." I turned around, and she'd climbed up and was standing on the seat. I was more freaked out than she was because I got a good look at the snake, and it was a big one. I shot it, but that time it was a little too close to her for comfort, and I don't think Jess realized the danger she was in.

Early on I didn't get paid much. There were times, even after Jess and I got married, that I had to borrow a couple hundred bucks to make it through the month. Before we married, I really didn't have that many expenses. But after the wedding, expenses went up. Money was tight from the very beginning, and we hadn't thought much about money when we decided to get married so quickly. I guess we thought our love for each other would carry us through. But it was tough and started to cause some friction between Jess and me. Duck Commander was a successful, growing company, but no one was making a lot of money back then, and I was making a little over minimum wage.

When we started arguing about money, or anything else, Jess tended to say a lot because she liked to get everything out on the table and deal with disagreements head on. But when I got mad or upset, I would always go quiet. I liked to think about things and take time to figure out what I thought, so I'd walk away and shut down, which she called the silent treatment.

Or if I was really mad, I might break something. I've been known to knock a hole in the wall. A lot of times I'd just get mad because I was trying to fix something and couldn't get it to work, like the time I couldn't get the air-conditioning filter to go in, so I punched a hole in the wall of our brand-new trailer. Another time I bumped my head on the towel rod in the bathroom and got so mad I ripped it out of the wall.

Once, our friends Gary and Erica were coming over. Jess and I had just finished the worst fight, yelling and intense. I was standing next to the stove, and I put the hammer fist down on the thin stove hood and crumpled it in. After I punch something, I always immediately feel better. I've never hit Jessica, though, and I never will. But hitting something seems to be my way of releasing tension.

When Gary and Erica walked in right after I beat down the stove hood, I stomped out and said, "Y'all have fun. I'm out of here. I'm driving to my mom's."

Whenever Jess and I had a fight, I always said I was going over to my mom's. She'd say the same thing—that she was going over to *her* mom's house.

While I was on my way to my mom's, Gary called me on my cell, got me to meet him somewhere, and we had a good long talk. Marriage was turning out to be harder than I thought it was going to be.

"I thought it was going to be more fun than this," I told Gary. "I think I might have made a mistake."

Gary nodded and seemed to understand.

We didn't have money to do things we wanted to do. We disagreed sometimes on how to spend the money we did have. And I also had a hard time with seeing men around town Jessica had dated or even seeing how men looked at her sometimes. It fired up my jealousy and the insecurities I had about whether I could trust her to be loyal and faithful to me.

Every few months those fears would return almost in a cycle, and I'd get mad, get quiet, and stop talking to Jess. We were two strong personalities dealing with some tough stuff from the past, and while Jess had told me everything, I still hadn't told her everything I'd been through. I held on to some secrets, and that might have been part of what fueled my anger.

About six months after the wedding, Jess got pregnant. We knew we wanted to start a family, and we both wanted a big family, but I was surprised when it happened and hadn't really planned for a baby yet. As soon as we told my dad, he started in again, telling me the story about my own birth in 1978. Mine was the only childbirth experience he's been a witness to, and I believe he regrets the decision although Mom made it clear she wanted him in the delivery room when I was born. And I don't think he'd ever do it again. But he never wastes an opportunity to bring up the horror he experienced when I was born as he watched, especially when someone new is standing nearby.

"I'll never forget the day I saw you come out of your mother's womb," he says, emphasizing each word. "The tearing and the blood . . . as I saw this boy come forth."

I always jump in, laugh, and say, "That's so gross," because I think it's the reaction he's looking for, and it shortens the story. But it never stops him from telling it again at a later date.

We found out Jess was pregnant in an unusual way. I was in the duck call room, working on wooden duck calls with an old rusty knife. A wasp flew in, and I picked up a flyswatter with my right hand and started batting at the wasp. I missed the wasp but somehow stuck the rusty knife into my wrist. I was concerned, knowing there are some veins in the area, and showed it to Dad, but he didn't think it was a big deal. Within minutes, however, my wrist had ballooned up to the size of a lemon, and it was obvious I'd hit a vein with the knife. It got real ugly and looked like a busted hot dog weenie.

I went home to Jess, and she took one look at my wrist and immediately drove me to the hospital. While being treated in one of the emergency rooms, I started shooting the breeze with my brother-in-law, Andy, who was on staff at the hospital as a nurse practitioner, and then all of a sudden, Jess disappeared. I looked around, and there she was—crumpled up on the floor. Andy went over to check on her.

After a few minutes I began to wonder if I would bleed to death in the meantime, but she came out of it, and so did I. The nurses helped her sit up, and she quickly woke up again. She seemed sleepy, though, and we were both distracted by my wrist. Andy said she could be pregnant. Later that week she took a pregnancy test, and it came up positive. Jess was super excited, and I was in shock. I couldn't believe I was going to be a father when I was still trying to get used to being a husband.

TWENTY-TWO

An Unbelievable Miracle

Jess

Children are a gift from the LORD;
they are a reward from him.

—Psalm 127:3 NLT

AS SWEET AS MY JEPTHA IS, AND AS MUCH AS I LOVE HIM, MARRIED LIFE in the trailer wasn't always easy. Yes, we'd chosen to be with each other and, in front of our families, had committed to each other for life. No question. But marriage was still hard. Although I was a new creation in Christ Jesus, I was still worried, people-pleaser me. My self-esteem seemed to come and go, and I would start feeling insecure again. When Jep got jealous or felt insecure himself, it was hard. Really hard. But this time I knew Jep was the one I was supposed to be married to, and I loved him like crazy.

Most of the time things were good. Jep and I were like best friends and spent the majority of our time together. One thing we completely agreed on, and always agreed on, was starting a family. And we both wanted a large family. My sister had experienced some trouble getting pregnant, and I knew that it could take a couple of years for me to get pregnant, so we started trying in February.

When I wasn't going down to Duck Commander with Jep to help out, I helped Korie out with some babysitting. Willie and Korie's son, Will, was a baby at the time, and Korie worked at the church, so I used to go up to the church and watch Will during the day. The first month went great. I still loved babies, just like when I was a little girl, and little Will was adorable. But by the second month I started feeling sleepy all the time. I could not seem to stay awake, and I started thinking something might be wrong with me, so I made an appointment with my doctor.

Before I could get to the doctor, though, I got a call when I was up at the church with Will. Jep had somehow stabbed himself in the wrist.

"It will be fine, son," Phil had said, telling him to put a Band-Aid on it.

But it wasn't fine. His wrist started swelling up, and it looked disgusting by the time he got home. It turned out to be okay—he'd nicked an artery—although it was good we got him to the hospital when we did because it was bleeding pretty good inside. But while he was sitting on the table in the examining room, with my nurse practitioner brother-in-law draining his wound, all of a sudden *I* didn't feel good.

"I feel like I'm going to throw up or pass out," I said.

I started to go down, sinking into unconsciousness, and everybody left Jep and came over to me. I didn't faint because of Jep's hand—I don't get grossed out at stuff like that. But something was going on, and when I woke up, I was so sleepy I felt like I'd been drugged.

My brother-in-law Andy, who was on duty at the time, asked me point blank, "Could you be pregnant?"

A little later I called my sister-in-law Missy, who at the time worked at the women's clinic, and she told me to come on up and get a blood test. I did, and guess what? It came back positive! We almost couldn't believe it. Just two months of trying to conceive and we were already pregnant after just seven months of being married! I was super excited, Jep was excited, and Miss Kay was excited. Once I knew what was causing my sleepiness, I took better care of myself, got plenty of rest, and started to feel better.

Jep and I went back to our normal routine, but I quickly started to realize that Jep is kind of a worrier. He was always worried about the baby. For example, if we went to the gas station to fill up the car, he'd worry about the strong smell of the gas and how it might affect our unborn baby. I think he was starting to realize that our lives were going to completely change. He was beginning to think about becoming a dad, and just like he took marriage very seriously, he also took becoming a father very seriously.

In the summertime, at twenty weeks gestation, I started having some back pain. It got worse and worse, and my back went into spasms with horrible nerve pain down one side. I didn't know what was happening but later found out I was having premature contractions. I wasn't sure if this was normal or not, but I had a feeling it wasn't good. Finally, Jep and I realized the pain wasn't going to stop, so we went to the hospital.

The pain continued, and I began to realize my situation was serious and our baby could be in danger. I tried to stay calm on the outside, but inside I was terrified. I was afraid not only for the baby, but the excruciating pain kept getting worse. This was like nothing I'd ever felt before, and I got to the point where I couldn't handle it anymore. Then the bad news came.

"We need to stop the contractions," said the doctor. "If you dilate, we won't be able to stop it, and we won't be able to save the baby."

They put me on morphine and magnesium, and I stayed in the hospital for three days while they worked hard to stop the pain and the contractions. The medication worked, but Jep and I worried it would hurt the baby. At least she was safe, for now.

After the three days, I was able to go home, and Miss Kay and my mom came by to visit and brought homemade food. Jep had to go back to work, so friends came by to help, too, and brought fun little things—magazines and toenail polish—to lift my spirits and help me pass the time. But it was hard, and Jep and I worried more and more. We prayed for the baby, but it was hard not to worry about her. *Is she going to make it to full term? Will she be okay? Will my morphine treatments affect her?* And my worst nightmare: *Is the pain going to come back and start up the contractions again?*

I went to physical therapy to try to relieve the back spasms, and the pain started up again. It was excruciating, and I had to go back to the hospital for IV fluids to make sure the baby was still getting the nutrients she needed. To be honest, that fall is mostly just a blur. Family got me through it, and I don't know what I would have done without them.

The holidays finally rolled around, and I wasn't able to do much, but my back was feeling a little better. As the due date got closer, Jep and I weren't as worried about losing the baby. We still worried about the effects of the medication on her. Doctors decided to do a C-section and scheduled the delivery for December 26, two weeks before her due date.

We had planned to spend Christmas morning with my family, and then head over to Phil and Kay's for Christmas night. The whole family was there, including all the grandkids. Bella, Willie and Korie's daughter, was the youngest and still an infant. We opened presents, ate dinner, and the whole evening felt surreal. *Tomorrow morning I'll have a baby in this world*, I thought. When Jep and I left that night, I said, "I'm gonna go have a baby. See you all later!"

For all the worry and concern and tears and prayers we'd spent on our unborn baby, when it came to her birth, she was no trouble at all. I went to the hospital, got prepped for the C-section, and within thirty minutes she was out. Lily was beautiful and healthy. I was overwhelmed with happiness and joy. I felt God had blessed me. He'd created life inside of me—a real, beautiful, breathing little human being—and brought her into this world through me. It was an unbelievable miracle. And the best part? Jep was in the delivery room. Unlike his dad, he wanted to be there, and he shared it all with me.

I'll never forget the sight of Jep decked out in blue scrubs, with the blue head cover, holding his baby girl for the first time. I'll never forget how she nestled down in the crook of his arm, his hand wrapped up and around, gently holding her. He stared down at her, and I could see a smile behind his white surgical mask. He was already in love—I knew that look.

After we admired the baby together, I fell asleep, and Jep took his newborn daughter out to meet the family. He told me later *he* bawled like a baby. Later, when she went to the hospital nursery, Jep kept going over there to stare at her. I think he was in shock and over-whelmed and excited.

Lily had a light creamy complexion and little pink rosebud lips, and she was born December 26, 2002. Despite the rough pregnancy, she was perfect. God answered our prayers, and now we were a family of three. We'd been married just a little over a year.

We brought Lily home, I bounced back quickly, and the pain was gone. Something about that particular pregnancy didn't agree with my body but, thankfully, I never had those same issues again.

I was so happy. I had changed lots of diapers in my twenty-two years and cared for lots of babies, but our Lily was ours, and to us, she was perfect and healthy. She was easy and quiet, and she slept really good. I always knew I was going to love being a mom, and I was right. I loved it. I could even take her to the movies, and she wouldn't make a peep.

Phil always says Lily was the first granddaughter who wasn't afraid of him. And it was true. From the very first time they laid eyes on each other, baby Lily was a match for Phil. She just took to him. I guess it was the beard, and it was a good thing Jep had a hunting-season beard when she was born because she was used to it. She loved her Papaw Phil, and as soon as she was a few months old and could sit up, she'd sit in his lap and watch Fox News. Jep had always said he wanted his children to be around his family, especially his parents, so I made an effort to bring Lily down to Phil and Kay's as often as possible. While Lily sat with Phil, I'd help Miss Kay with work or in the kitchen or just sit and visit.

In the back of my mind, I still carried some of the fear and worry from my pregnancy. As she got closer to a year old, Jep and I noticed Lily hadn't started talking yet, although she seemed to be normal and healthy in every other way. She was alert and sweet and smart, but she was quiet. Her eyes were big, and she watched everything going on around her. But she didn't talk.

In her second year, we got a little more worried because Lily still wasn't talking. Developmentally, everything else was on track. She grew and ate solid food and crawled and walked, but still no words. We were concerned and afraid something might be wrong.

Lily finally started talking when she was three, and she has turned out to be as smart as can be and does very well in school. There is nothing wrong with her. Lily is on her own timetable, and we had to wait patiently for her personality to emerge. I'm guessing her quiet personality came from her dad. I don't know, but maybe I did all her talking for her, and she didn't feel the need those first few years!

Lily is twelve years old now. She's still sweet and smart and quiet, and she still loves her family.

TWENTY-THREE

Through the Lens

Jep

Don't wait for something big to occur. Start where you are, with what you have, and that will always lead you into something greater.

—Mary Morrissey

I LOVED BEING A DAD. I WANTED TO BE A HANDS-ON DAD AND BE AROUND for all of the important moments of my kids' lives. Jessica and I talked a lot when we were dating and first married about having a family and how we wanted to raise our kids. Granny and Pa had such an influence on me, and we were so close, that I wanted the same thing for my kids. I can't imagine life without my grandparents. Jessica felt the same. So early on, when Lily was still small, we tried to be down at my parents' as much as possible. It's a different way of life down there—casual, no big plans, and eventually a big meal happens, and we tell old stories. I hope I never take it for granted.

Not only did I want my kids to learn good Christian principles early on from my mom and my dad, but I respect how my parents raised me to behave and to respect my elders. I don't want to get "preachery," but some of the kids I see don't have any respect for their parents. It breaks my heart. I was taught to respect my elders. The following dialogue happens often.

Me, responding back to someone: "Yes, sir."

"You don't have to call me sir."

"I can't help it. You're a sir to me."

It's awkward, and nowadays we forget a lot of that stuff. Manners and respect are overlooked in my generation. I want my kids to respect me and to respect Jessica, just like I was taught to respect my parents and grandparents. My parents were consistent, and even though I didn't always like the discipline, because my dad didn't put up with any crap, I respect it now and appreciate the lessons I learned.

As much as I respected my dad as a disciplinarian and wanted to follow his lead, I also wanted to be a loving father. I wanted to have both and to always show my love to my kids by hugging them, spending time with each one, and saying "I love you." I won't ever call my kids idiots.

I don't hold anything against my dad because when he grew up, it was tough, they didn't have much, and that's all he knew. My granny told me about how kids were never allowed to talk around adults. You couldn't even ask a question, or you'd immediately get a wooden spoon to the top of the head. When they ate, kids always ate last. If there was one piece of tomato left, that was all you got. If you asked for more, you got whopped with the wooden spoon. I'm sure Granny was tough, but she had to be with Dad and his brothers.

When we were kids, if we did something that wasn't bad enough for a whipping, Dad would thump me hard in the head, and sometimes the pain would make me cry.

"Don't be an idiot," he'd say. I thought it was normal.

I want my kids to both love and respect me. It's the same with marriage and a relationship with God. If you don't fill your relationships with both love and respect, it's going to be a tough life. I try to, and I fall short, of course, but I think hard and often about those two goals. From what I've seen, if you can master those two components of a relationship, your wife and your kids will respond. I discipline my kids, but we also love on each other.

––––––––––––

Just eighteen months after Lily was born, we had our second daughter, Merritt. Born on July 30, 2004, Merritt was named after Granny, whose first name was Merritt. Two years later, on August 4, 2006, we had Priscilla. And two years after that we had our son, River, born on December 5, 2008. I was a blessed man with four beautiful children and a smokin' hot wife. But as much as I loved my family, I also felt the burden of supporting them.

As our family grew, our bank account seemed to shrink. I struggled to support my family, and Jessica did what she could, too, getting her Realtor's license along with making and selling children's clothes. We moved out of the trailer and into a small place closer to town and finally bought a small piece of land and started building a house.

As the money pressures mounted, I started thinking about finding a new job. I'd always worked for Duck Commander, but I felt maybe it was time to do something else, learn a trade and not be so dependent on my family, as I'd been doing my whole life. Spiritually, I always leaned on my family. But economically, I wasn't sure if I should keep doing that, so I talked to my brother Alan, and he listened.

"Why don't you pray about it? Then maybe you should go make your own way."

As a company, Duck Commander was doing okay, but there were struggles. Both Jess and I were stressed about money. Day care was expensive, and there were times we couldn't pay the bills. Six people living on a low salary? We were barely making it. We accumulated some medical debt—it seemed like the kids were sick all the time—and some credit card debt. There were times I had to borrow money from Duck Commander to pay the bills and make ends meet. There were also times our parents helped us with groceries. At one point it got so bad we were looking at foreclosure on the house we'd built.

I thought about going to work on the offshore drilling rigs, down off the coast. It was hard work but paid well, and my pa, along with Jessica's dad, had both made a good living doing it. My dad had worked the rigs for a while too. I also thought about going to work at the paper mill in West Monroe. I even interviewed for a job selling copy machines.

"We want you," they said. "We can't pay you as much as you're making at Duck Commander, but you can work your way up."

No, thanks.

Eventually, I talked to Dad and Willie about my plan to go work on the oil rigs. Both told me to stay with the family at Duck Commander.

"That would be a mistake," Dad said. "Stay with us. You won't believe what's going to happen in two or three years. Be patient."

He had faith in the business, and he felt it was just a matter of time until we hit it big.

"We're all going to do well," he'd say.

Did I mention he's one of the most optimistic people you'll ever meet? Every day we go hunting (and he hunts every single day of duck season), he'll sit back, laugh, and say, "Boys, this is going to be the best day of our life. You'll be telling your grandchildren about this day!"

Willie felt the same. "You've got to do what you've got to do," he said. "But let me tell you this, I'm fixin' to turn this thing around, and I want you to be here for it."

I decided to stay because Jess and I knew it was more important to be with family than to make more money. I continued working just about every job at Duck Commander. I still loved shipping and packaging, and I watched the entire run of *X-Files* episodes when I worked in that department. Then I started making the reeds, the job Uncle Si does on the show.

———

When I was a young kid, Dad got the idea to film some of our duck hunts. He hired Gary Stephenson, a local science teacher, to make the first video, *Duckmen 1: Duckmen of Louisiana*, back in 1987. Over time the VHS videos, and later the DVDs, caught on and began to sell as hunters and hunter wannabes realized they could enjoy hunting with us without ever leaving their living rooms.

Then one day in the late nineties, when we were out hunting with a different cameraman, Greg, one of Alan's best friends, he handed me the camera.

"Just turn it on, and ask your dad how the hunt is going."

Then he showed me how to turn it on, focus, and zoom.

A couple of weeks later, I went hunting again with Dad and Greg and ended up picking up the camera several times. I remember filming some decoys. "Hey, I'm shooting B-roll," I joked. Greg was really nice and always encouraged me.

One time, I remember grabbing the camera on a whim and thinking, *I'll see if I can get a duck coming in.* It's not easy to film a duck on the wing. They move quickly, sometimes unpredictably, and I have to contend with the changing light, the weather, the trees and vegetation, and the other ducks, all of which can get in the way. Different species fly a lot faster than others. For example, teal, the small ones, can really book it. So Greg taught me how to keep the camera in focus.

But on this day, the duck, a big mallard drake, circled up above us and came in nice. It was the first time I'd ever filmed a duck, and I got him pretty good as he came toward us with wings out kinda wide. I zoomed in, and he filled the lens, my heart beating fast. *Whoa. Here he comes!* I got really fired up. Later, when we watched the footage, I was as excited as if I had a gun in my hand. It was a cool feeling; I was hunting with my camera. The other guys liked what I'd done too.

"Jep, that's really good," Dad said.

After that I started picking up the camera more and more, but I just did it randomly, so I never got paid. It was so much fun. Dad's friend, W. E. Phillips, was the one who told me to think about taking the filming more seriously.

"Jep, I'm tellin' ya, you need to start filming more. You could have a career here. You can do these odd jobs, but making these DVDs might be a good idea for you. You'll miss hunting season, but you can make a good future for your family."

"I guess I'll try it," I answered.

I'd always loved art. My high school art teacher, Miss Sharp, the best teacher ever, always encouraged me.

"Look, you can do this," she'd say whenever I got frustrated.

She always stayed after class and never got tired of answering my questions or helping me get the effect I was after. I really got into it, including joining the art club, and I won several awards. I think the whole reason I got into videography later was because of her encouragement, and she teaches art to my kids today.

As a young kid I was obsessed with movies. I'd watch a movie with a friend and notice the camera angles. I'd say something to my friend, but he never understood. I'm visual, and I like artsy movies and cool perspectives. I probably get some of it from my mom, who's made some amazing paintings. It seems to come easy to her, especially wildlife.

"I think I'll paint a duck today," she'll say. And she does.

Deep down, art had been a dream of mine. I've always enjoyed going deep on projects and doing something that takes hours and hours of work to accomplish. Video became a creative outlet for me, almost like an obsession, just like when I'd run those endless basketball drills in my front yard or worked out for hours in the gym when I was a teenager.

As I got better and better behind the camera, I started thinking up creative ways to capture the action. *We're gonna get something no one has ever seen*, I'd think. I started trying to get impossible angles or over-the-shoulder stuff with unusual perspectives so the viewers felt as though they were actually there in the duck blind with us.

In all I worked for eight seasons, filming our duck hunts, and I ended up not only shooting video but also directing and editing as well, and getting paid something for it. Some of my shots were unique and weren't duplicated by anyone. A lot of it was from practically growing up in the duck blinds. I could tell by the way my dad blew a call, and how the ducks were responding, where I should focus; it was just instinctual. At the time no one else could capture ducks on camera like we could. As technology progressed over the years, cameras were smaller and even more responsive. I missed hunting a little bit, but I remember plenty of times coming home from work and telling Jess, "You won't believe the shot I got today."

After a while we started adding in footage of us talking, telling stories, and messing around. We all got comfortable with a camera on us. Uncle Si was always a big talker and storyteller, but he never liked the cameras, and he wouldn't tell his awesome stories if he knew the camera was on. So we started hiding the cameras. I'd put a jacket over it or set up a camera behind a gear bag so Si wouldn't notice it. It helped that the cameras were smaller. When we finally started capturing some of his stories on video, Si saw how funny he was, and he didn't get mad. I'd always told my friends, since I was a little kid, how crazy my Uncle Si was. Now they could finally see for themselves.

The Duckmen videos became more and more popular. Our biggest ever was *Duckmen Five: Traditions*. Here's what was written on the back of the box:

> Many men spend a lifetime struggling to possess what a few men are born with. Join Phil Robertson and the Duckmen and see not only duck hunting, calling, and shooting, but see also their heritage and what makes the Duckmen so unique. Feel the danger and excitement when you come face to face with alligators and cottonmouths . . . with some it is just hunting. With Phil Robertson, it is a way of life. Lock, load, and hold on.

We took *Duckmen Five* to the big outdoor show in Memphis that year, and we sold them things like crazy. I'll never forget sitting in the hotel room with Mom and a pile of cash on the bed. It was about a $20,000 mound.

"We finally did it! We went big time."

We were so excited. After that the DVDs were even more popular. At first, only the hardcore hunters watched them, but over time they caught on with a larger audience, and we knew lots of kids watched them. Then the Outdoor Channel came calling. It was time for the Robertson clan to lock, load, and hold on because we had no idea what was ahead for us all.

TWENTY-FOUR

Stitched with Love

Jess

Never underestimate the power of a woman with a sewing machine.

—Unknown

I LOVED BEING A MOM TO MY THREE GIRLS AND MY SWEET BOY, AND I loved everything that went with it. Except for the fainting. Just like with Lily, I fainted each and every time I got pregnant, except with Priscilla—I didn't ever faint with her. I also drank a bottle of castor oil with Merritt because she was overdue and someone told me it would help me go into labor. (And yes, I found out the hard way that you're only supposed to take a little bit. Now I know!)

The craziest fainting spell happened when I was pregnant with Merritt. I was about three months along, and we were in Las Vegas for the Shot Show. It wasn't long after the terrorist attacks of September 11, 2001, and the security lines were so long. I woke up extremely thirsty that morning and kept trying to drink water. At the airport, waiting in those long lines, I kept telling Jep, "I'm hot. I need water."

"Come on, we'll get some later," he said, trying to get us and our stuff through the lines.

I was feeling worse though. "I'm going to throw up," I said.

I didn't want to throw up in front of all of those people, but I didn't know what to do. The only thing I could figure out was to go to the edge and throw up over the railing to the floor below because there didn't seem to be anyone down there. Just then we were somehow separated, and Jep was in a different line. His line was moving faster, and he got ahead of me.

All of a sudden I started blacking out. I couldn't see anything, and I was holding the rope.

"I think I'm passing out," I yelled.

As I dropped to my knees, a stranger crouched down beside me.

"Ma'am, are you okay?" he asked.

"I think I'm passing out."

"Is that your boyfriend ahead?"

I guess he'd seen me talking to Jep or else saw him looking back at me with a worried look on his face.

"No, my husband."

Then I heard Jep's voice calling out. "She'll be all right. I've seen her do this. Just roll her over on her side and put something under her head. She'll be fine. Roll her over so she doesn't choke on her tongue."

No one would get out of line to help me. The man beside me called out for a doctor.

I heard someone reply, "Yeah, I'm a doctor."

But even he wouldn't get out of line.

Missy quickly came to my aid and asked, "Can you breathe?"

And yes, Jep did eventually come back to check on me. The feeling finally passed, and I felt better, but not before the entire family left me behind. I had to hurry to catch up to them in the other section.

With River, our youngest, I was playing tennis during the summer. It was about 100 degrees, and with the humidity it felt like about 110.

"I'm seeing stars," I told my friend. "I'm gonna sit down now. I feel like I'm going to pass out."

By now I was familiar with the feeling, and I knew it was because of being pregnant, so I didn't worry. "It's just a heat thing. I can't breathe. The heat got to me. Just bring me some water, and I'll be okay."

When I told Jep what happened, he said, "You're not playing tennis anymore because you're carrying my baby."

Even though I learned not to worry about fainting when I'm pregnant, I do tend to be a worrier. My mom is a major worrier, a hundred times more than me. My grandma is too. I want to break that cycle.

Being a mom can be scary, especially when you hear stories about terrible accidents or psychotic people who hurt others. Whenever I'm away from my kids, I always think in terms of a worst case scenario, and it's hard for me to leave my kids for any reason, including dates with Jep. I love them so much and worry so much that sometimes it becomes overwhelming. I want to just keep each child with me all the time, but I know I can't do that. I want my kids to grow up and try new things and live their own lives. Just not yet.

The way I've learned to deal with the worry is through prayer. I don't want to burden Jep or the kids with all of my worries, so it helps that God knows my heart. I know God is in control, and I ask Him to protect my family in every way. I pray throughout the day whenever my kids come to mind or whenever a worry pops into my head. I even stop and pray when I see an ambulance go by. Deep down, I know I'm not in control, so it does no good to worry. I'm okay with the fact that I am weak and God is strong, so I'm grateful He is in control.

The other thing I've always worried about is our finances, and I worry more as I get older and feel the responsibility of providing for our children. When our debts began to mount up and there didn't seem to be a way out, I knew I needed to work hard to find a way to bring in some extra income but also to try and stay at home with the kids as much as possible. I never wanted to be a full-time working mom. Being rich has never been important to me—I've always wanted to be rich in love, and with a large family, I am.

When we were first married, Jep might have made more money working somewhere else, but I loved that he was working with his family, eating a home-cooked lunch at Miss Kay's table every day and getting fed spiritually. I think he would've quit if I would've said okay. But when we talked it over, I just couldn't agree.

"Don't quit. You may not make a lot, but you're with family," I told him.

He decided to stay at Duck Commander. It wasn't until he started working as the cameraman that we didn't have as many financial struggles.

Meanwhile, to bring in some extra money, I earned my Realtor's license and even went to school for a while in prenursing. But my favorite job during those years was with the Matilda Jane clothing line for children. I've always had a knack for putting together colors and textures, and I've always loved fashion and design, so I funneled that into a sales job as a "trunk keeper." I put together home shows known for beautiful clothes, a warm atmosphere, and good food. I worked really hard and became pretty successful. I felt really blessed, and we were able to pay the bills a little easier.

I loved quilts and fabrics and thread and buttons long before I ever actually sewed anything, and I love my family quilts, as well as quilts I've found in antique shops. When I was a little girl, I fell in love with my grandmother Lola's sewing room, bursting with everything a seamstress could ever dream of—thread in every color, brightly patterned scraps of fabric, jars of buttons, pincushions, and bolts of fabric.

Out of her sewing machine came beautiful dresses for my mom and quilts for her children and grandchildren. She died when I was just nineteen years old, so I never got the chance to learn the craft from her. But I did inherit my love of sewing and quilting from her and the value of tiny scraps of fabric that can be recycled into something new and beautiful.

After I took my first sewing class, I started making quilts. When they turned out nice, and people seemed to like them, I began making original clothes for local children's boutiques, along with baby quilts, diaper bags, and car-seat covers. One popular item I came up with was jackets made from vintage handkerchiefs.

It wasn't until Lily was born that I wanted to make baby clothes, so I took another sewing class. It was a magical time, when those first sweet little dresses emerged from my sewing machine, as I learned how to do smocking, tucks, and lace inserts for girls' clothing. As soon as my girls were old enough to hold scissors, I taught them how to cut fabric into blocks for us to piece together into family quilts for them to keep so I can pass along my love of quilting, and my grandmother's love of quilting, to the next generation.

Jep's granny was a quilter and a knitter. She kept her hands busy, and when I knew her, she was always sitting on the couch, knitting something. She knitted an afghan for every new grandchild, and Merritt got two afghans because she was named after her great-grandmother.

I want to pass on a legacy of creativity and of taking something that seems of little value and transforming it into something beautiful. Our quilts are like our lives, each with a different story, each a little tattered and torn, but each unique and beautiful in the way the patterns, colors, and designs come together. Quilting is becoming a lost art that I never want to lose. To me, quilts are the perfect combination of love and art.

TWENTY-FIVE

Secrets

Jess

Nothing makes us so lonely as our secrets.

—**Paul Tournier**

JEP AND I HAVE BEEN CRAZY ABOUT EACH OTHER FROM THE VERY beginning. From our chance meeting at Connie Sue's to the Bible studies, baptisms, and our summer romance, something always seemed to draw us together even when others were trying to keep us apart. We also both had emotional scars and baggage to deal with, and those difficult feelings kept reemerging from time to time through the first seven years of our marriage.

We didn't fight all the time. We didn't even fight a lot. But about every six or seven months, things would get hard. We absolutely loved each other and were committed to our marriage, but we really struggled with forgiveness and with moving on and not bringing up the past when we fought. It was like a crazy carnival ride that went around and around, and no matter how hard it was or how tired we got, we couldn't seem to get off.

Sometimes it was so hard I started to be afraid that maybe our marriage wouldn't work. When things were hard or we were in a fight, Jep would disconnect. It's like he was present but not present. Or he'd get jealous after running into some guy I'd once dated. These tumultuous periods always left me feeling really insecure. *Am I a good wife? Will he always love me? Am I enough for him?*

The quiet was hard for me to deal with. I always wanted to talk everything through, and Jep's withdrawal and the not-talking made me fall back into my old patterns of blaming myself and feeling ashamed and worthless. I felt our conflicts were my fault for the bad choices in my past, and I wondered if it would always be this way. But maybe the silence was best because the hardest moments were those when he'd say, "This just isn't fun like I thought it would be," or "I just really don't love you." Those moments were devastating, and the words stayed with me in my heart and continued to hurt, long after they were said.

The next day he would follow it up with, "I'm sorry," and we'd move on. But at my core I felt Jep might never completely trust me because of my past. I knew early in their marriage Phil had expressed some jealousy toward Miss Kay and had accused her of cheating on him.

I had a best friend to confide in, and that helped; but it was hard because I loved Jep with all my heart, and I knew he loved me. I just didn't understand why we had to go through these periodic emotional upsets.

When I looked back at my first marriage, the worst advice I got from friends was, "God would never want you to be unhappy." I've found that no matter how much you love someone—whether it's your husband, a family member, or a friend—he or she will eventually let you down. And when you are let down, you are open to those lies about how your own personal happiness is the most important thing in life.

Most marriages that I'm aware of are challenging at times. And many of them come to a make-it-or-break-it point, when the hurt is so bad and so deep, it seems you cannot endure it and it's time to give up and walk away.

"You don't deserve this" or "God wouldn't want you to be in this situation" are other comments I got from friends during my first marriage. I know those people loved me and just wanted me to be happy. But I should have been listening to God back then, not to people. One thing I've learned about marriage is this: everything good comes from hard work and fighting for something. Marriage takes hard work, and at some point you will have to fight for it. Commitment to marriage brings glory to God.

So I fought for our marriage. God gave me enough strength through our emotional ups and downs. Sometimes when I felt overwhelmed and needed a sense of peace, I sang a song to myself about Christ calming the storm and how the waves would obey him: "Peace, be still." I also had Phil and Miss Kay to thank, in part. I knew their story and how they stayed together through very hard times when most people would have bailed. I think that's why God has blessed them so much. They still give all the glory to God, and they reach out to help others who are struggling. They know life isn't just about them and their personal happiness.

For seven years I treaded water, trying to be a great housewife. I was blessed to be a mother to four wonderful children. I worked hard to help with our finances. And I tried to stay positive and know that when things between Jep and me got bad, the moment would pass if I could just hang on.

But then our make-it-or-break-it moment came. It was in 2008, after our fourth child, River, was born. I came home, and I saw something I hoped I'd never see. I walked in on Jep, and he was at the computer viewing pornography. I stood there for a moment, frozen, because I literally could not believe what I was seeing. Then I gasped, turned around, and walked straight out. *I can't believe it*, was all I could think. I was numb.

I jumped in the car and drove straight to my grandmother's house in Arcadia. On the way I called my mom and told her I needed to drop off the kids, but I didn't tell her what happened. I just couldn't say it out loud yet. I cried on the way, and I cried when I got to Mamaw's house. I couldn't bring myself to say anything, and I remember her eyes looking so sad for me.

"I don't know what happened," she said. "But we love you."

Later that evening I called my best friend from Mamaw's house and said the only words I could think to say: "It's over. That's it for me." I'd been walking on eggshells for so long, trying to be strong and make our marriage work. I'd had a feeling there was something going on, but I never knew what it was.

I'd always blamed myself and thought it was my past and my wrong choices that were a continuing source of conflict in our marriage. It almost seemed as though Jep had put himself on a pedestal, blamed me for my sinful past, and put me through hell at times. Now I suspected—and would soon find out that my suspicions were true—he'd been struggling our whole marriage with an addiction to pornography. I felt completely rejected. *I'm just not worthy of love*, I thought. It was my worst nightmare coming true.

Is he keeping any other secrets from me? Now that I had discovered this one, I just figured he'd been lying the whole time we'd been married, and I was sick of playing the fool and turning a blind eye because I didn't want him to leave me. I was angry. But I was also hurt and feeling insecure all over again, just like in high school. *Yep, you're not good enough . . . pretty enough . . . important enough. You're ugly. He doesn't want you. He wants someone else who looks just like those girls.* The same old lies came back—and strong. I hated those feelings, and it made me want to harden my heart again so no one could hurt me.

I finally drove back home late that night and went to bed without talking to Jep. I felt weak and damaged. I just couldn't get warm, and I felt sick. The next nine or ten days were all a blur. I was keeping up my routines and taking care of the kids, but I was hurt and numb.

Once I got over the shock of finding out, the anger and the hurt rose to the surface, and I know I hurled some very angry words at Jep. I felt betrayed, and I lashed out, wanting him to know how bad I was hurting.

"Am I not good enough for you? Am I not pretty enough that you have to look at other women? Aren't I enough?"

I couldn't even begin to think how we could overcome this. I still felt our marriage was over and this was something I could not forgive. It was a betrayal that hit me where I was most wounded and vulnerable.

For a while life went on. Jep went to work every day. I was busy nursing baby River and taking care of three other small children, two of whom were still in diapers. Jep and I didn't talk a whole lot, and the atmosphere in our house was quiet and somber. For most of the time we kept it cordial. We would still talk some, but things were different. I didn't feel close to him, and I wasn't even sure if I wanted to be in the same house with him anymore.

I wanted and needed sympathy, and my sisters in Christ helped me to feel not so isolated. Deep down, I knew God had brought us together, and I didn't want to be apart from Jep, but I was so hurt I didn't know if I could go on.

One night Jep and I were meeting at my parents to pick up the kids. They were inside, and Jep got there first. He met me on the front porch, before I could go inside, and told me to sit down. I really didn't want to hear anything he had to say. I was still hurt, angry, and closed off. But I didn't really have a choice, so I sat down and looked at him.

When I looked at him, I could feel his hurt even through the brick walls I'd built around my heart. Jep was in pain. I could see it in his eyes.

"I need to tell you something," he said.

His voice was shaky, and what he said next was something I never in a billion years expected him to say.

TWENTY-SIX

The School Bus

Jep

He heals the brokenhearted
and binds up their wounds.

—Psalm 147:3 NIV

THAT NIGHT WAS THE HARDEST NIGHT OF MY LIFE. I'D GOTTEN TO Jessica's parents' house before she did. I remember sitting in the grass to the side of the porch, alone, and weeping. I knew our marriage was in trouble. I knew I'd done something very wrong and had been doing it for a good while. And I knew I'd hurt the person I loved the most in this world.

In a way, I was relieved that my secret struggle was out in the open. I didn't have to pretend anymore. But I was also afraid this was really the end of our marriage and my relationship with Jessica. And if it was the end, I wanted her to know it all. I wanted to get everything out in the open. I didn't really think much beyond that. *Whatever happens, happens.*

There's certain stuff you don't ever want to go back to, but as I sat there alone, the memories flowed over me. I'd been a little kid and confused. I remembered weird things, like how she smelled and how I threw up outside the bus. It was bad, real bad. She tortured me and hurt me. I rolled around in the grass before Jessica got there, crying. *Do I need to bring that memory up?* I felt nauseated and miserable as I waited for Jessica to get there to tell her. *I can't keep it a secret any longer.*

"I need to tell you something," I said to her when she arrived. She looked at me silently, a question in her eyes. I was embarrassed and looked down, then continued. "I've never told anybody this." I looked back up and felt tears at the back of my eyes as I started to tell Jess my story.

"It started when I was six. I used to ride the school bus home from school. There were kids my age on the bus, but there were also older kids. Some of the kids from West Monroe High School would ride the bus up to Pinecrest then transfer to another bus to West Monroe. Most of the kids got off the bus before it got to our neighborhood, so there was hardly anyone on it at the end.

"An older girl started sitting next to me. She seemed sweet at first. She'd come sit beside me, like a motherly figure almost. I remember her being sweet and taking care of me. I liked to sit in the back so she'd come sit with me."

I looked over at Jess, but she wasn't looking at me. She looked straight ahead or down. Anywhere but at me. I kept talking.

"After a while the girl started doing strange things. She'd take my hands and push them up under her shirt and tell me I was tickling her. Then she started making me pull down my pants. It was awkward. I didn't know what was going on, but I knew something wasn't right.

"It didn't happen every day. Sometimes she left me alone. But it did happen regularly, and I became more and more confused and scared. I moved to different seats and even tried sitting up by the bus driver, who didn't seem to have a clue what was going on.

"I didn't tell anyone because I was embarrassed and ashamed. Finally, school let out for summer vacation, and I didn't have to see her anymore.

"The next year I was seven years old. On the first day of school, I remember thinking, *I don't want to be by that girl again.* I knew something wasn't right, and I didn't want any part of it. But she was more aggressive this time. Whenever we were alone on the bus at the end of the line, she touched me and made me touch her.

"Soon the threats started, whenever I tried to avoid her: 'I'm gonna kill your parents if you tell anybody,' she'd say. 'I'm gonna come and kill you, your mom, and your dad.' The sweetness she'd shown the year before was completely gone, and she turned dark and threatening. Her language was filthy, and I didn't know what most of the words meant. I was scared of her and didn't know if she'd follow through on her threats or not.

"I still didn't tell anyone, and I didn't see a way out, so I started pretending I was sick some days so I didn't have to go to school. My mom didn't know why.

"Finally, whenever we were alone on the bus, I'd walk up the aisle and stand right by the bus driver. At first, she told me to go sit down because it wasn't safe to stand up.

"'Please, please, Miss J, can I just be up here by you? Please!'

"And that's how I finally got out of it. It happened for a couple of years, and I never told a soul. It was weird and confusing and scary."

I finally looked at Jessica again in the dim porch light. I had no idea how she would react or if she would think I was trying to get sympathy or manipulate her. It was a secret I'd held for too long.

It wasn't exactly true that I'd never told anyone. I had told one person—a good friend I'd gone hunting with a few years before. We'd been driving down the road just relaxing and talking, when our conversation got really serious and he told me about being molested as a kid. My school bus experience came back to me, and something made me tell him about the girl on the bus. I'd buried the memories, but they came flooding back. It was strange—after we talked about it, I felt better. My buddy understood the feelings because he had been through it. Some of the shame and fear I'd been carrying inside for all of those years was gone, and it felt like a heavy weight was lifted off of my chest.

I should tell Jessica this, I remember thinking. But the moment had passed, and I hadn't said anything. Until that night at her parents'.

Now it was all out in the open. Jess knew everything. I sat and waited for her to say something. She had listened carefully, but she wasn't crying, and I wasn't sure what she was thinking.

"Why haven't you told me this?" she asked.

I don't remember what my answer was, but I knew why I hadn't told her. I was embarrassed and ashamed, and I just wanted to forget it and pretend it had never happened. But it had, and something had prompted me to tell her the truth. It was probably bad timing, sitting there on her parents' porch when our marriage was a mess because of me, but I wanted to get it all out there. Maybe it was meant to be, and if I was completely honest with her, there was a chance our relationship could heal. All I knew was I didn't want to lose her. She was the best thing that had ever happened to me. I needed her, and I was scared to think I had pushed away the one person who loved me most and was the best friend I'd ever had.

TWENTY-SEVEN

Forgiveness

Jess

When you forgive, you in no way change the past—
but you sure do change the future.

—Bernard Meltzer

AS I LISTENED TO JEP, I DIDN'T FEEL MUCH AT ALL AT FIRST. IT WAS AN awful, horrible story, and I reacted like a mother. I have always been super careful with my kids, and I've always worried that something bad would happen to one of them. Some people are sickos. How could anyone want to hurt an innocent child? I was angry that this teenage girl would do something like that to a boy. I wanted to protect him, to go back and save the little boy he'd once been from that girl.

After a while it began to sink in that someone had hurt my husband, really hurt him. My defenses were up, so I didn't want to show any emotion to Jep. I didn't really even want to feel any emotion, but

I did. It moved me when he broke down and cried. Deep down, I still loved him, but our marriage was in a serious crisis, and at this point it was very hard to open up my heart to him and try to give him comfort. I was still angry and very, very hurt.

But this was something different . . . a type of wound that I didn't really even understand, but I knew we'd have to deal with it if we were going to stay together and if our marriage was going to have a chance of surviving. In a way, it seemed like another huge problem to deal with when I felt I already was hanging on by a thread. But I also knew it had taken a lot of courage for Jep to tell me what had happened to him. I know that sexual abuse happens not only to girls but also to boys even if it seems men don't talk about it often. I wasn't sure where we were going from here, but I was glad he'd told me. I just needed time to process it, and I knew I couldn't do that alone.

After that night things began to change between Jep and me. We started talking a little more, and I didn't feel sick to my stomach as often. We talked to Alan and Lisa about everything, and that helped since they'd been through some similar struggles. (You can read their story in their book, *A New Season*.) It also helped to talk to a good friend whose husband had also struggled with a pornography addiction. Ultimately, I had to decide whether I was going to forgive Jep or not. What he'd been doing had been very hurtful and disrespectful to me. I wanted us to love and respect each other and to be in an open, honest relationship.

First, I started with my thoughts, and I made a conscious decision to forgive Jep. I couldn't pretend I had never done anything wrong in my life. I had, and I'd been forgiven, by Jep, by the Robertson family, and, most importantly, by God. So I knew what it was like to be forgiven and to have a fresh start in life. How could I not allow Jep to have that too?

I started thinking about my vows and my responsibilities as a wife. *What if I leave Jep and he turns to drugs and alcohol and abandons the Lord? What will happen to him? If I leave, will there be another woman in his life? Do I want my kids calling someone else Mom?*

Over time I began to look at Jep more as a soul than as a husband. I cared about his future, and I wanted him to stay secure in his faith and his walk with God. It was my heart's desire to do everything I could to help Jep and my four kids get to heaven by showing them Christ in me. And I knew I couldn't do that if we were apart.

I started praying for God to bring our relationship back to life. *Lord, help me to fall in love with him again,* I prayed. And slowly, surely, it became more about God than about me or Jep. We finally put God at the center of our marriage, and He not only restored our love for each other, but He made that love deeper and stronger than ever.

And I wasn't perfect either. I knew I didn't have the power to hold our marriage together or to change things between Jep and me. I had tried my best to make it work and to fix things but was unsuccessful. I finally understood I was scarred and flawed and broken. Who was I to think that I could fix another broken human being? Or a broken marriage?

Ultimately, this is what I realized: God must be the center of our marriage. And both Jep and I have to love God even more than we love each other. That's the only way it's going to work and the only way our marriage is going to survive. God is the glue that holds our marriage together, and I've learned that if I seek Him, He answers. He heals all wounds—not in a day, maybe not even in a week—but He cares, and He can put relationships, and people, back together in His own time and in His own way.

TWENTY-EIGHT

Just Ducky

Jep

Faith, family, and facial hair.

—**Jep Robertson**

JESS AND I ARE REBUILDING. WE'RE REBUILDING OUR RELATIONSHIP and rebuilding our lives, and we're committed to keeping God the center of everything we do. It's not easy, it never was, but it is best. And our marriage is stronger than it ever was.

Forgiveness isn't easy; but when you realize we're all broken and we're all works-in-progress, then it's a little easier to extend grace to others—especially when you remember the grace that you've been given through our Lord and Savior Jesus Christ.

We all are going to sin along the way. We're going to mess up and stumble and fall. But it's how you react to sin that makes the difference. Being honest, open, and humble about your mistakes is the way to go. The people who truly love you—your family and your friends—will love you and forgive you and allow you to make a fresh start.

I've also learned that staying close to my family and my friends here in Louisiana is helping me to become the man God made me to be. It's easy to get caught up in the fast life, but I want to live a godly life, and I want God to use us to help bring other people closer to Him. That's why Jess and I do the show. We love *Duck Dynasty* because we get to work together and share our lives and our faith with others. And that's a great feeling.

Being on a reality TV show is a strange and unusual way to make a living, but it means Jess and I get to work together. And I'm still working, as I always have, with my family. We work long hours, and there are strains that go with making a living in the entertainment industry. And trying to make time to go to church and see friends can be a strain when we don't really have control of the filming schedule.

I take being a provider seriously, and that made the success of the Duckmen videos, and my video work, very satisfying. But when the television opportunities came knockin' on the door of Duck Commander, leading to *Duck Dynasty* becoming the highest rated cable show on television, I was as surprised as anyone else. Excitement and fame and recognition and money all come with the success of the show, but what makes me the happiest about it all is the opportunity to provide for Jessica and Lily, Merritt, Priscilla, and River. Knowing that I can feed and clothe them, put a roof over their heads, and put some money in the bank for their education is what keeps me going. I'll never be as well-known as my dad, or as well-off as Willie the CEO, but that's all right. The show has been a blessing, and I'm grateful for it.

In addition to giving me a job that provides for my family, the other thing I love about *Duck Dynasty* is the opportunity to spend more time with my family. Dad and Mom mostly stay down at their place on the river, Alan was busy pastoring a church, Jase was with his kids when he wasn't working or hunting, and Willie was always on the go.

Since I'm the youngest, my kids are younger than my brothers' children, so even though we lived in the same town, we wouldn't run into each other at school or sports games very often because of the kids' age differences. We still got together as a family for holidays and saw each other at church, but we all were busy working, hunting, and raising our families. *Duck Dynasty* is a blessing because it brings the Robertson clan together, and that is always good. We still argue and tease—everybody gets teased in our bunch, and I've had it my whole life, being called the baby sister and all—and there is no substitute for a great Uncle Si story or a smile from my mom or a random but wise observation from my dad.

The show really is an extension of our lives, and we pretty much do what we've always done and how we've always done it, except now there are cameras, lights, sound equipment, cords, and crew members around. Oh yeah, and millions of people watching.

One question I always get about the show is why I wasn't on much in the first season, which concentrated more on Willie, Korie, Mom, and Dad. Actually, it was planned that way. We are a big family, and we all kind of look alike with the beards, so the idea was to introduce us slowly so people could get to know us and our different personalities.

The show was originally more centered on Willie, always known as the CEO, and his adventures running the Duck Commander family business, with all of the strong personalities of the family as a backdrop. From the first few shows it became clear that as funny as my parents and Willie are, Uncle Si was the one with true star quality. Audiences quickly fell in love with his quirkiness and his crazy stories, and even though early on in the Duckmen days he was the one who hated the camera the most, he grew into his new role as America's crazy Uncle Si.

As crazy as my Uncle Si is, though, he's an incredible storyteller and that plays well on camera. Once he gets into a story, you're hooked, and you can't wait for him to finish, no matter how long the story goes (and sometimes it goes looong). They're the same stories we've heard over and over for years in the duck blind, with Dad telling him to be quiet, but now the rest of the world can laugh at them too. Some of his stories have definitely changed over time—he'll say something happened in Germany when he used to say it was in Alabama.

"Si, didn't you say it was Alabama?"

"No, it was in Germany."

End of argument.

When I was introduced and started appearing on the show, I was always labeled "Willie's other brother" since Jase, or "Willie's brother," showed up first. You could spot me once in a while in the duck call room or at family dinners, but I wasn't featured regularly until about season four. Jess was on camera more than I was, and I realized I needed to do something to set myself apart, so I started reminding everyone that I'm Mom's favorite. There's a favorite in every family. I just happen to be the one in ours.

When I did start appearing regularly, and viewers thought I was funny, I took right to it even though I was more used to being behind the camera. I wasn't ever nervous—none of us really were—and I think it's because we're just playing ourselves, being ourselves, and we're doing it with the people we've been around all of our lives, right in our homes and our regular hangouts. I'm used to the cameras, and I just try to come up with great lines to get back at my brothers for all their mistreatment, except my sarcastic revenge lines get to happen on TV for the ultimate in public humiliation.

One of my favorite episodes is where I beat my brothers in an all-day strength contest, including eating hot peppers, playing a spring-loaded board game called Perfection, and pulling a monster truck across the parking lot. Of course I beat Willie and Jase, no problem. Even sweeter was when Willie hurt his back trying to pull the truck. (We won't mention the we-are-poor-sports-so-let's-get-back-at-the-little-brother-by-duct-taping-him-to-the-pole incident, however, that happened afterward. I'm still trying to grow the hair back on my arms.)

While the show has become our jobs, *Duck Dynasty* has also affected our lives in other ways. During the filming season, our schedules are demanding, and it's hard to make plans or live our lives apart from the show. Sometimes we're traveling to do promotional work for the show, and I miss the kids, or we can't make it to church, so it's always nice to be on hiatus and get back to a normal schedule. We've been filming two seasons of the show a year, so it's almost like we lead two parallel lives as a family—one where we're on call and have to always be available for shooting with some long days, often apart from Jessica and the kids, and the other life where we can settle into a more normal family routine and just live our lives. But no matter how tough a filming day can be, I'm grateful, and I look at it as getting paid to have dinner with my family. I am blessed.

I've also realized, now that I've been blessed with a good paycheck, that I think I'm like my dad, and I really don't care about money so much. It doesn't make you happy. I had a great childhood, and I never even had my own bedroom. What does make you happy is doing for other people. Whether it's taking fresh deer meat or ducks to some neighbors in need down the road or flying down to the Dominican Republic to help build an orphanage, it's people that matter, not money.

When I went to the Caribbean with Korie a while back to help build the orphanage, I came with bags full of new Hanes underwear and T-shirts. When I handed out those little packages, worth just a few bucks each, the kids literally fell to the ground, crying with happiness. They were the happiest, funniest little kids, grabbing my beard and smiling big. They have nothing, and some free underwear made them happy.

It was a big wake-up call for me as I realized how much I have and how a little inconvenience like the Internet going out can ruin my day. I don't want to live like that, like the world owes me a comfortable life and I'm not happy unless I have all the conveniences. I want to live a fulfilled life, and I want my kids to live a fulfilled life too. I want more for my kids. I want to show my kids how to have faith in Jesus, how to use the Bible as their guide to life, and when they grow up, I want my kids to change the world.

I also want Jess and me to continue to learn how to love each other, and I want us to grow old together and be just like my mom and dad. My idea of happiness is being with my family in a cabin in the woods or at a campout, sitting around a campfire telling stories, roasting marshmallows, and watching the fireflies.

TWENTY-NINE

Family over Fame

Jess

You don't choose your family. They are God's gift to you, as you are to them.

—Desmond Tutu

JUST LIKE JEP, I LOVE BEING A PART OF THE *DUCK DYNASTY* SHOW. I DID have a choice to be part of the show or not, but I'm blessed to be part of the Robertson family, and I felt blessed to be part of the show with them. Our motto is "Faith, Family, Ducks," and *Duck Dynasty* is something we've all done together. Jep and I gradually grew into the show, rather than just being thrown in. During filming season, it's nonstop four- to six-day workweeks for the cast, so as a mom of four, I've been able to still be a mother and wife while becoming part of a television show.

Being on camera was more nerve-racking for me than for Jep. I didn't want it to seem as though I was nervous at all, and being surrounded by my husband, kids, and my in-laws made it easier. After a while I forget the cameras are there, and the family dinners are especially fun when one or more of my kids are involved and I get to spend several hours just hanging out with them. I wouldn't want to be anywhere else in those moments.

But our work doesn't stop with filming. Now that we're on the show regularly, there are other opportunities coming our way. I receive lots of phone calls, and we have all kinds of business proposals to consider and try to make wise decisions on, especially as we think about a future beyond the show. One of the first things I did when we started working on the show was to open savings accounts for each of our children. I let them spend only a little of any money they earn; we're teaching them how to save even though they're still young.

Jep and I also get asked to make personal appearances. Sometimes it's a photo opportunity, where they want us to dress up and appear on a red carpet somewhere. But lately we've been getting asked to speak, too, and to tell our story. It wasn't easy for Jep at first—he's more of a private person and the thought of getting up in front of hundreds or even thousands of people and telling his story was pretty scary. I remember the first time he spoke to a large group was in Canada, and he was holding the mic and shaking. But everyone listened, and every time he has done it, it gets a little easier.

Same for me. I'm a people person, and I love to talk and share stories, but speaking to a huge crowd is not easy. Both Jep and I try to remember that we're just talking. I sort of ramble all over the place, and I don't always know where I'm going when I talk, but Jep is so much better at it. People take what he says to heart. There's something built in to Phil and Jep that makes people listen to them. They share moments and memories from their lives, and people love it. Jep always had it in him.

When we're off-season and not filming, Jep and I love to cook

Phil with baby Jep, playing on the floor after a long day at work.

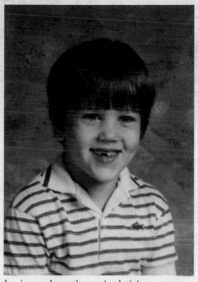

Jep in an elementary school picture.

The boys learned at an early age how to pick ducks. (Left to right: John Gimber, little Jep, Jase, Jim Gimber, and Willie)

Jessica with her big sister, Stacy, in New Orleans.

Jep and Santa, aka Johnny Howard.

Jep and Jessica, all starry eyed, dating and having a good time in Destin, Florida.

Jep with his brothers on his wedding day.

Jep and Jessica's wedding day, simple and magical.

Jep and Jessica's first ski trip together, just two months after saying, "I do."

Jep in his infamous plaid pants when he introduced himself to Jessica at the Edge of Madness.

Shot Show in Las Vegas, a little work and a little R&R.
(Left to right: Howard Carbo, Lisa, Bill Philips, Korie, Willie, Missy, Kay, Alan, Jessica, and Jep)

Lily, the first born, with Jep and an adorable matching Mohawk.

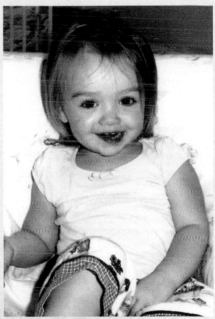

Lily has always had a sweet spirit.

Jessica with Merritt in the dress Jessica made for Merritt's baby blessing.

Granny, the original Merritt Robertson, and baby Merritt.

Jessica with Priscilla at three months.

Priscilla is Jep and Jessica's third angelic baby girl.

Merritt, a little ballerina.

The family at Easter before River was born.

River was a charmer from the start—look at those dimples!

River with Jep at the pumpkin patch.

Merritt, Priscilla, and Lily, all dressed up for a little trick or treating.

Jessica is glad to have her man home after a long day of hunting.

The wives at the Robertson family's annual beach trip.
(Left to right: Lisa, Korie, Kay, Jessica, and Missy)

Every beach trip includes the men playing several rounds of golf.
(Left to right: Alan, Willie, Jep, Jay Stone, and Jase)

Jep and Jessica have felt
especially blessed to have had
these four babies.
(Left to right: Priscilla, Lily,
Merritt, and River)

The Robertson family's annual beach trip.

Jessica with a few of her closest friends.
(Left to right: Jessica, Melissa Dasher, Erica Osborne, Darcy Fisher, and Jil Dasher)

Jessica and Emily Decorte quickly became best friends after meeting in 2005.

Everyone needs a family sunflower picture.

together. I mostly talk, and he mostly cooks. I don't like to cook that much anymore—I did when the kids were little, the first seven or eight years we were married. Then Jep started cooking, and now he cooks, and I clean up after him, and that works great. I also love small moments together with Jep—having coffee, going to the gym and running on the treadmill side by side, or taking a walk or a car ride. Sometimes I pick him up from work, and we go get a bite to eat. We're together a lot, and we love it.

Jep's always been a romantic, creating scavenger hunts for me to find gifts on special occasions. On our first anniversary, he sent me on a scavenger hunt to find a KitchenAid mixer. One time after being away, I came home to flickering candles and rose petals scattered on the floor and a brand-new outfit he had picked out for me, complete with shoes and jewelry. Last Christmas he sat me down on the couch and asked, "Do you want your Christmas present early?"

"Sure," I said.

"You're sitting on it."

I looked under the cushion and found a big manila envelope, which led me to an envelope in the freezer. The next one led me to the grill outside and a few other places around the house. I finally ended up at a picture of Miss Kay that hangs on our wall. Taped to the back was a little box with a beautiful pair of diamond earrings inside.

The show is a part of our lives, but it's just a part. Our lives are more about our faith in God, our love for each other, and the family we are raising together. You know, if God wasn't for us, we wouldn't be where we are today. Because we love God more than we love each other, we've been able to overcome the hurts and the scars of our younger lives and build a new life, centered on Him, focused on faith and family rather than on ourselves.

And even though we sometimes fly here and there and do things famous people do—to do our part to support the show—in the end, I love being at home. Most of the time I wish I could just sit in my house all day, with a quilt on my lap, enjoying Jep's cooking, catching a rerun of *Golden Girls* or *Murder, She Wrote*, playing cards with the kids, and enjoying my family. Fame is fleeting, but family is forever.

THIRTY

Smackdown

Jep

We rejoice in our sufferings, knowing that suffering produces endurance, and endurance produces character, and character produces hope.

—Romans 5:3–4 ESV

I'VE ALWAYS BEEN PRETTY HEALTHY—PROBABLY THE WORST PAIN I'VE ever felt was with my hernia when I was playing basketball. Until the pilonidal cyst, that is. Not to make this a woe-is-me story, but it was more painful than I imagined anything could ever be. And it went on for a year. They're weird little creatures—just a gap in the skin right above your tailbone. I'm not quite sure what causes them. But when I was nineteen or twenty, I had one of these cysts flare up and get infected. It hurt, brother!

I had to go into the hospital and have it worked on, and then the doctor packed it with gauze and I-don't-know-what, which had to be changed daily. For a year. It was excruciating. I couldn't sit down, and it was even painful lying on my side. Maybe in the end, it was a good thing—it happened after my family intervention, and maybe it helped me stay out of trouble. I do know I leaned on God to get through it. After a year of very slow healing, I was finally pain-free. Other than my broken ankle in high school, that was about it for any medical problems. A hernia and a cyst. Not a big deal.

Maybe my number was up for something major because in October 2014, I got a huge smackdown, physically speaking. I was on a big hunting trip with Buck Commander, a company my brother started that revolves around deer hunting and other big game. I love those guys, and we're all good friends. We hunt together every year. Three years ago I killed my biggest Louisiana buck there. Some of the Buck Commander partners are country music guys and baseball players. There are camera guys—I bond a lot with the camera guys—and I bring a friend or two along sometimes. You can bond when you're all in a hunting camp together.

I got to camp on a Friday night, and we went bow hunting Saturday morning and didn't see much. We saw a good buck on Saturday night, but it was too late, so I was hoping to get a shot at him on Sunday evening. Evenings are better there for buck activity for some reason. So the next day three of us headed out to a deer blind out on a big greenbelt, where the deer come out and graze in the evening, woods on either side. We were about twelve feet up in a prefab plastic and fiberglass blind. It's big and very comfortable. We got out there about two-thirty in the afternoon and got all set up and ready, hoping to see the buck. A half hour later we saw him, about six hundred yards away. The buck worked his way toward us, grazing leisurely. Eventually, at about six, he came almost within range. With a bow, the deer have to be pretty close, but the buck was still about seventy yards out. It was a long shot, and there was no way I could get him. I was itching to get off a shot, but then he started easing off to the right and away. We were disappointed. It wasn't going to happen that night, and I set down my bow.

We had about thirty minutes before it was dark, so we stayed there and just relaxed, enjoying the evening and joking about the one that got away. We started making some plans about setting up a ground blind the next day, and then it was time to pack up and get back to camp. I remember strapping on my backpack . . . and that's the last thing I remember, so I'll let my buddy Matt tell the rest of the story.

Matt

It was me, Jep, and a cameraman named Curly in the redneck blind. We got out to our blind earlier than anyone else, and we told stories, trying to whisper and laugh as quietly as possible. The deer were in the food plot, and it looked like it was going to be good, but then the does left the field, and the buck didn't get close enough, so it wasn't going to happen.

About six-thirty, it was too dark for the camera, so we decided to head back. I was the first one up. I packed and climbed down the ladder. I was down at the bottom waiting when I heard a loud bang up in the blind, like someone had fallen over hard. *Thud!* At the same time I heard a loud, uncontrollable groan. It made the hair on the back of my neck stand up. I knew something bad had happened.

I threw my stuff to the ground and was back up in the blind within seconds. I stuck my head inside and saw Jep lying on the floor, Curly standing next to him. Jep was convulsing, his head jerking back and forth, eyes rolled back, mouth open, and arms and legs jerking uncontrollably. I immediately knew what was happening—I'd seen a woman have a grand mal seizure just a month before.

My first thought was, *Is he joking? Is this some big joke?*

"Curly, what just happened?" I said, my eyes on Jep.

"I don't know. He just fell!"

Curly bent over and tried to protect Jep's head from banging into the side of the blind. There wasn't much we could do. The violent seizure seemed to go on forever, but it probably lasted four or five minutes. We tried to keep Jep from hurting himself, and then we just had to wait until it was over. Finally, it stopped, and he ended up curled up on his side in a ball, unconscious.

Curly and I discussed what to do. We knew it was bad—I didn't even know seizures lasted that long—and we needed to get help for Jep. But it was dark; we had no vehicle, no cell coverage, and it was a mile back to the lodge. We decided I would go for help and Curly would stay with Jep. I climbed back down the ladder and started running up the gravel road to the lodge. Halfway back I got super winded and walked for a bit. I had a little cell coverage and tried to call Willie, but there was no answer. I assumed everyone else was still in the deer blinds with their phones turned off. I started running again and finally made it back to the lodge.

"Hey! Hey! We need some help!" I shouted as I approached. No answer. I burst into the lodge and saw a couple of guys.

"Jep had a seizure. Call 911," I said, out of breath. "Somebody call an ambulance!"

I grabbed somebody and got into a truck, and we rushed back to the deer blind. Jep was still in the same position, curled up into a little ball. He didn't respond at all, and when I touched his head, he felt extremely hot. I took off my shirt and poured a bottle of water on it and draped it over his head. I thought it might help cool him down.

Somebody was able to text Willie. At first, he thought it was a joke. When he realized we were serious, he headed our way. We got word an ambulance was coming, but we knew it would take a while to get out to the deer camp, so we decided to get Jep back to the lodge, where he could be more comfortable. We tried to wake him up to see if he could get down the ladder, and he did wake up, sort of, but was very confused. We got him down the stairs, and before we could get him into the truck, he pulled out his cell phone and started punching buttons. I wondered if he was trying to call Jessica. He paced around restlessly, mumbling, but I couldn't understand anything he said.

"Jep, let's get you in the truck and back to the lodge," I said.

Somehow he heard me, and he walked to the truck and got in. Willie met us at the door to the lodge, but Jep didn't seem to recognize him. Jep was there physically but not mentally, and he looked confused and lost. Willie looked at me with his eyes wide. I'd hoped after the seizure that Jep would just wake up and snap out of it, but it was clear something serious was going on, and we all were getting pretty worried.

Jep walked inside on his own, but then it got really strange. He didn't seem to recognize anybody, he mumbled as if he was trying to talk, but he made no sense, and he kept walking around. At one point he saw his black camo face paint in the mirror and turned on the faucet and washed his face. He was only partially successful because his hands weren't working right. He tried to get a drink of water and accidentally spit some on the floor. Then he bent over and cleaned it up with a paper towel. It was almost like he was sleepwalking or on autopilot.

After that he kept walking around, bouncing off walls, and his motor skills seemed to get worse and worse. He wouldn't look anyone in the eyes, and he kept scratching his head and his beard, tangling his hair up until he looked like a madman. All we could do was try to keep him from hurting himself. This went on for about two hours as we waited for the ambulance to arrive.

My wife, Lexie, was with Jessica and the kids, and we'd been planning a big family dinner together for that night with barbecued steak and potatoes. At the very least, that wasn't going to happen, so I called my wife to let her know about Jep's seizure. I didn't want to talk to Jessica directly—I was afraid the worry in my voice would cause her to panic. I didn't want her to worry because although we thought it was bad, we didn't really know. I just wanted her to get to the hospital to meet Jep. Maybe he would recognize *her*.

Finally, the ambulance arrived, and then it got really crazy. Even though Jep didn't seem to be that aware of what was going on, he definitely didn't want to get into the ambulance and started fighting the paramedics. We tried to help, but Jep is really strong, and when he doesn't want to do something, it's hard to make him do it even when he's half out of his mind. Finally, Willie got on top of him and helped to hold him down so the paramedics could strap him onto the gurney, take his vitals, and get him loaded into the ambulance.

As soon as the ambulance drove away, all of the Buck Commander guys huddled up, about fifteen grown men in camo, all hugging and praying out loud for Jep. We were all choked up and fighting back tears. We didn't know what was going to happen to him.

THIRTY-ONE

This Is Serious

Jess

The Lord is my strength.

—Psalm 118:14 NLT

WHEN MATT CALLED HIS WIFE, THE KIDS WERE IN THE BATHTUB, HAIR still wet, and Lexie and I were trying to get them ready for bed so we could enjoy our steak and potatoes with the guys and visit around the fire pit. But as soon as we got the call, we went into emergency mode with the little information we had. I called my mom, and even though she was on her way to the movies, she made a U-turn and beelined it for home. Lexie and I loaded up the kids and dropped them off at my mom's. I told them I had to go check on Daddy, but I didn't want to worry them by saying anything else. I didn't really know anything else.

I called Willie and found out they were taking Jep to a little hospital near the deer camp.

"I just want to prepare you for what you're going to see," said Willie.

My stomach clenched into a tight knot of shock and worry.

"You're not going to believe it. I've never seen anybody act like this before. He's like a madman. He's fighting people. He doesn't know who we are. This is serious, and something is awfully wrong."

When I arrived, I walked straight into the emergency room, where they were manhandling Jep, trying to check his pulse and get an IV started. He was moving around, was restless, and couldn't seem to focus his eyes.

"Hey, Babe. I'm here," I said in a gentle voice.

I couldn't tell if he heard me. He looked at me but seemed to look right through me. He was elbowing the nurses and doctors. He looked like being touched was severely painful and cried out whenever he was touched. When it came time to wheel him back for a CAT scan, he started punching, and I thought he was going to take out the technician, a woman, with an uppercut.

It was chaotic, and doctors and nurses kept asking what medication he had taken because he was acting like a drugged-out crazy man. I kept telling them he hadn't taken anything. I knew he would never do that. I thought maybe it was some sort of reaction.

When he was in the scanner, he kept lifting up his head and banging it on the curved part of the scanner. I tried to help keep him calm, but I was afraid he was going to kick me in the stomach or break a rib. They were able to complete the scan, and it came back normal. His blood and urine also were negative for everything possible. Then they put a sedative in his IV to try to calm him down so they could transport him to the larger hospital in West Monroe. Lexie drove the car home, and I rode in the ambulance with Jep. I was in complete shock. It all had happened so fast, without warning, and I didn't know what was going on.

I'd heard a few stories from his friends already, and they were buzzing around in my head. Curly said that when Jep was trying to use his phone, he said, "Jessica," one of the few things he said that made any sense. Another story, that would have been funny in almost any other context, was that at one point Jep looked up and said, in a clear voice, "I have to get money from Willie." Another friend told me that back at the lodge, while they were waiting for the ambulance, Jep kept wanting to walk outside and head for the woods. I shuddered in fear at that story—the deer camp was in the middle of 55,000 acres of woods. If Jep had been alone and wandered off into the woods by himself, he might've been lost forever. When that thought came, I put my hand lightly on his arm. He was quiet, for the moment, still strapped securely to the gurney. *We might've lost you,* I thought. *We've been through so much together. I can't lose you now.*

When we got to the hospital in West Monroe, Miss Kay met us at the door. Kay walked up to the gurney as they rolled it into the emergency room and said, "Hey, baby, your mom's here."

Jep just looked at her, and it was clear he didn't know his own mother. I walked into the waiting room with her, where the rest of the family and some friends were waiting.

"It's not good," Miss Kay said to everyone in the waiting room.

And I knew it wasn't good. I was still in shock, and I didn't know what emotions to feel. I didn't know what to think. No one seemed to know what was going on.

Jep's childhood doctor was there, and he stayed and worked on Jep. They started testing him for anything and everything. They put him in the ICU and, because he was still violent and so restless and out of his mind he was strapped down to the bed, they decided to completely sedate him until they could figure out what was going on. Because he would be in a medically induced coma on heavy sedation, they had to put him on a ventilator, and it was hours before I got to see him again, and I hated that. I wanted to be with him every second because, honestly, I wasn't sure if he was going to make it.

They started pumping him full of antibiotics because it was possible he had some sort of bad infection. Then, finally, something good happened. One of his best friends, from the old kissing-bandits days, walked in. Blake is a neuroradiologist and was off duty but came in when he heard what was going on. From that point on Blake came around to see Jep whenever he could, monitoring his records and helping us understand what was going on. He became Jep's advocate at the hospital, and I felt like God had sent Blake to us to be Jep's guardian angel during the ordeal.

It was a long night with no real results or answers, and Monday morning dawned with Jep unconscious on a ventilator and Miss Kay and me hovering nearby. I didn't want to leave his side, even for a second, and I kept my hand on his arm, his head, and even his foot whenever I could. It made me feel better and seemed to calm his movements. I also talked to him constantly and tried to explain what was going on although I didn't know if he could hear me. I just wanted him to know I was there by his side.

We finally got some results early Monday morning. A lumbar puncture showed a high white-blood-cell count, and doctors thought he might have viral meningitis. They also decided to check him for encephalitis, a deadly brain inflammation caused by an infection carried by mosquitoes. It wasn't good news, but it was a relief to know that it was potentially treatable and it wasn't a brain tumor or something like that.

Miss Kay was pretty positive, or at least she acted that way, and I held it together pretty well on Monday. But Tuesday one of the doctors seemed concerned and said it seemed like Jep had a little pneumonia settling in. The word *pneumonia* was a red flag for me. I immediately flashed back to when Papaw was in the hospital. He'd been sedated, too, and contracted pneumonia and died. And that's when it all got real.

All of a sudden, I couldn't look at Jep anymore. I didn't know if he was going to make it. The thoughts came fast, overwhelming me. *I love him. And I don't want to live without him.* I started thinking about the future. *If he survives, and gets over these deadly infections and wakes up from the coma, what will he be like? Will he be able to talk? Will he know me? Will he know his kids?* That made me cry, the thought that he may not even know his own kids. *What will I tell them?* And then the worst thought of all. *What if I don't come home with my best friend?*

My life had completely changed in just two days. Sunday had started out being a normal day, with church in the morning and plans for dinner with friends in the evening. Now we were in the hospital, waiting to find out if Jep was going to stay with us or not. In the middle of all of this, Blake popped in again. I was never so happy to see anyone in my life. I started telling him what was going on, all of my fears and worries pouring out. Blake listened then left to look at the x-rays. He was back again in no time with news: "There's no pneumonia."

"What?" I said.

"Jep's going to be fine. He's going to come out of this."

I'd held in all my feelings. I'd tried to be strong and not let discouragement and the not knowing get me down. But I'd almost lost it when I'd heard the wrong diagnosis of pneumonia. Blake was there at just the right time, and he helped give me hope that it was all going to be okay. And he was there on his own time, not getting paid.

Over the next couple of days, Jep continued to receive more than a dozen different types of antibiotics in an effort to kill any bug inside his body that might be causing an infection. Doctors also tried to lower the level of sedation, but every time they took it down just a bit, he would start getting restless and violent again, trying to pull out his IVs. So they had to keep the sedation level high and his arms tied down. Even though Blake had given me some hope, I was still very, very worried. I prayed with the family in the waiting room, but most of the time I was in the room with Jep, holding his hand and telling him I loved him.

Finally, on Wednesday, they began to lower the sedation again, and immediately he reached for the ventilator tube and tried to pull it out.

"Don't fight it," I told him again and again, trying to explain what was happening. I held his hand. The nurse came in and told me they were going to try to take the ventilator out.

"Do you want me to stay, or leave you?" I asked him.

His eyes were closed, but he put his hand out and rubbed my back. Just for a moment. *He's there!* I wanted to shout. *Everything's going to be okay. The antibiotics must be working!* I wanted to sing and shout and dance.

After the ventilator was out, he began opening his eyes just a crack when someone came in to say hello. And things got even better—he was calm although he was still tied down, and when a friend and Willie came in to say hello, Jep said, "What's up?"

I wanted to laugh and cry at the same time. Those were the first words I'd heard him say since he'd gone deer hunting. I questioned him a little, wanting to know what he remembered, but he couldn't talk much and still seemed very sleepy, dozing off every few minutes.

Thursday morning was one of the best days of my life because Jep woke up bright-eyed.

"Why am I in here? What happened?" he asked.

He didn't remember anything.

He looked awake and alert and rested. But I was exhausted, having gotten very little sleep or food and not knowing if Jep would live or die, while he'd been taking the longest nap of his life.

We held hands, and though I was exhausted, I was happy. Thursday afternoon he talked a little more and ate a cracker. He was back. Slowly but surely, he was coming back. He knew who I was, so I believed he would know who the kids were. And he started talking more and more. *Thank you, Lord, for bringing Jep back to me.*

The news about Jep's health crisis began to leak into the community, and one tabloid media outlet got a tip and threatened to take the story public, so we knew it was time to share the news. Korie helped us by writing a simple press release:

Earlier this week while deer hunting, Jep suffered from a seizure. Thankfully, he was in the stand with friends, and Willie was at the hunting camp when it occurred, so he was by his side in a matter of minutes. He is doing well now, but is still in the hospital for additional tests and observation, and he is being treated with antibiotics to cover a range of possible infections believed to have caused the seizure.

Most major media outlets covered the story, and people around the world began immediately to respond with prayers and good wishes on social media. When Jep heard what was going on, he jumped on Twitter and tweeted this on Saturday from his hospital bed:

Well, I about died this past Sunday . . . I'm doing much better now. Thanks for all the prayers! #seizuresuck #gladtobealive

As if that wasn't enough, he also posted a side-by-side photo of himself and a bearded Steven Seagal, both unconscious in a hospital bed and wrapped in a white sheet. "Just like Steven Seagal, I'm hard to kill," it said in a caption at the bottom.

It's always a good sign when you get your sense of humor back.

Monday morning, most of Jep's doctors said he could go home. One of his doctors wanted him to stay for a month, but Jep wanted out. I didn't blame him.

We walked out of the hospital together. Jep could walk, but he was very weak and wobbly. On the way home we stopped to check out the house we were remodeling, and then I got him home to rest. The next day he asked, "When are we going to go look at the house?"

"We went yesterday," I told him. He didn't remember.

I let the kids stay home from school that Monday, and we had a wonderful time just being together. There were lots of hugs and smiles, and Jep played cards with River. I noticed he was talking a little slower than normal, but he was talking. And I knew everything was going to be okay.

THIRTY-TWO

Glad to Be Alive

Jep

Just like Steven Seagal, I'm hard to kill.

—**@jepduckman / Twitter**

I COULDN'T WAIT TO GET HOME. I WAS FOGGY FOR A FEW WEEKS AFTER, and I had a few headaches, but I recovered pretty quickly. I was covered in bruises though. I guess I earned those by fighting with everyone. I heard the stories—I elbowed a male nurse in the chest so hard I caused a big bruise. I slapped a paramedic in the ambulance. And apparently I even kicked Martin between the legs. *Sorry, Martin!*

Willie said at one point I balled up my fist, and he backed away, knowing he was about to get sucker-punched in the face. He was afraid if that happened, he'd hit me back, and he didn't want to do that since I was clearly out of my mind. *Brothers.*

Doctors still aren't sure if I have epilepsy or not. Time will tell. But probably the worst part about the whole experience is that in the state of Louisiana, you can't drive for six months after you have a seizure. I do know I'm lucky to be alive. My story could very well have ended in a different way. I could have fallen out of the deer blind and broken my neck, wandered off into the woods, or never have woken up out of the seizure. But here I am. I'm alive. Jessica and I are together, and we have our four kids and our families and our remodeled house. I want it to be the last house we ever live in. It's down the street from my brothers' houses, and behind us is green grass going down to some water, where I can watch the ducks swimming by.

Jessica and I have had a lot of hurt in our lives, and I've learned that you have to keep growing and learning how to love and respect each other and how to trust each other. There's no such thing as instant healing, but the hurts get easier with time, and the healing is faster when you face the hurts together.

THIRTY-THREE

Love Always and Forever

Jep and Jess

PHIL AND MISS KAY HAVE LEFT A LEGACY OF LOVE FOR THEIR CHILDREN and grandchildren. They've been teaching us their whole lives what Christ has taught them about love, sacrifice, forgiveness, and grace.

We want to carry on the Robertson legacy with our old and new friends, including those who know us from the television show.

It's a little scary to know we're being watched, but we look at it as a privilege to be able to show who we are and how we live our lives to so many others. We work hard to love each other and love others.

But in the end, it's our children who are most important. We want to carry on our family legacy with our four children and someday our grandchildren and great-grandchildren. It's an awesome responsibility to be parents and to know that what we are doing with our kids will have eternal consequences because we know this world is not our home—we're just passing through.

Yet even though parenting is a huge responsibility and a lot of work, it's also true that Lily, Merritt, Priscilla, and River have been the biggest blessings we've ever experienced. God's goodness shines through their eyes.

Our lives have been filled with love and laughter and lots of fun, but there have been stumbles and struggles and tears too. Life is complicated, but we know that if we continue to follow the Lord, step by step, He'll shine a light and lead us down the right path. He'll do that for you, too, if you only ask Him.

Once upon a time, a girl from town met a boy from the woods. And you know what? They lived happily ever after.

The end.

Well, actually, it's just the beginning!

Love always and forever,
Jep and Jessica

Questions and Answers

BEING PART OF THE *DUCK DYNASTY* SHOW HAS GIVEN US THE OPPORTU-
nity to share our faith and our lives with many, many folks. They have
become our friends, and as friends they want to get to know us better.
So we have chosen several questions that we are often asked and added
our answers for you, our newest friends.

Jep, what about the beard? Is it temporary or permanent?

JEP: My dad has had his beard for more than twenty-five years, and
he's never going to shave it off. The last time I saw his face was
in high school. My beard? I've thought about shaving it at some
point. But the last time I did, about six years ago, I thought I
looked so silly.

My beard used to be seasonal. I'd grow in a beard for hunting season and then shave it off although I always got real bad razor burn on the side of my jaw and my neck. My beard was splotchy at first and then finally filled in. Beards are good camouflage because ducks have sharp eyes. Also, the beard really does keep me warm out on the water or the four-wheeler when it's cold, damp, and windy.

If you don't have a beard, you have to wear something to cover your face. Here's my advice: *you boys, just grow a beard*.

Now the long hair, I could lose that. It's pretty uncomfortable in these Louisiana summers.

Is the hunting for sport, or do you really eat what you hunt?

JESS: We eat wild turkey, deer, ducks, quail, pheasants, and elk. Nothing is wasted. We eat what Jep kills, or we give it away to people who need it.

JEP: The only thing we kill that we don't eat is snakes. We try to get rid of as many venomous snakes as possible. I hate 'em. I really do. They scare me, especially with my kids out running around. A bite could be deadly to them.

The bad thing here is copperheads; they're everywhere. I had a friend walk out the front door of his house. A copperhead was sitting next to the front steps, and it struck him hard, biting his leg. He ended up in the hospital and survived with a bad scar. Cottonmouths make the worst scar; their toxic venom causes the flesh to rot. So we shoot 'em. The dogs help keep them away from the kids too.

Jep, now that you're famous, do you ever have women hitting on you? How do you and Jessica deal with that?

JEP: We do get subjected to flirting and to rude comments on social media, but I ignore them. Everyone just ignores those things. Jess and I have established certain boundaries so temptation doesn't become a problem, such as neither of us being alone with someone of the opposite sex, ever. There's no such thing as innocent flirtation. I want to avoid it and run away from any sort of temptation. You can't get into trouble if you're not there.

JESS: Both men and women say or do vulgar things to get Jep's attention, so we've decided he never travels alone. I don't want him to be tempted or to throw him to the wolves. Once an older lady grabbed his butt during a photo op. She did the same thing to Godwin. I guess she wanted something to go and tell her friends about.

Jessica, you seem really close to your mother-in-law. How do you get along with your three sisters-in-law since you were the last one into the family?

JESS: Missy and Korie grew up together, so they've known each other forever. Their kids are closer in age, so they got to spend lots of time together at games and school events. We were younger and had babies at home, so we usually weren't at those same events. Plus, everyone was busy working, raising their families, and living their lives. But once the television show happened, we started spending more time together on a regular basis, and we all grew much closer. I've always felt close to Lisa because Alan was almost like a dad to Jep, and they have given us great advice on marriage and parenting. I love all of my sisters-in-law and can't imagine being a wife and mom without their support and encouragement. I think that's why the show has been successful; it's a picture of a large family who loves and takes care of each other. The joking and teasing is all part of being a Robertson, and I love it.

Why aren't you and Jep in the introduction of the *Duck Dynasty* show?

JESS: This is always an awkward question. We can't all be in every shot or every promo because there are too many of us. Plus, we don't get a say in who's featured in the show. That's up to the show's creators, producers, directors, and writers. It's not important who is or isn't featured. It's not important who owns what or who is CEO of Duck Commander. We're all in it together, and we all support each other. We're family.

Jep, what has been your least favorite episode of *Duck Dynasty*?

JEP: I don't even have to think about that one. It's when I got taped to the pole by my brothers. That wasn't fake; it really happened. The duct tape was very tight, and I could hardly breathe. I was stuck there for about fifteen minutes, and that pressure—it was a pretty painful moment. And it hurt to take the tape off. People always talk about that and think it was funny. But for you older brothers and sisters, *do not tape your younger sibling to a pole!*

What's been your favorite moment on the show?

JEP: When my mom and dad renewed their marriage vows. My dad was so genuine; it really got to me. My mom has always loved my dad, showed it, and told him a million times. In return, he loved her and hugged on her and slapped her on the booty. But this time he actually *said* what he *felt*. He talked for a good long while about how she'd given him the best years of his life and got him through a lot of hard times. He said his life would have been very different without her. He also talked about his boys and how proud he is of us. He was honest, and I've noticed the older he gets, the softer he gets. He's always been a little hard and rough around the edges. Feelings seemed to be the last thing on his mind. Now he's more loving, gentle, and considerate. In return, Mom said she always wanted to marry a pioneer man, so she did, and she said she wouldn't take back anything. Jess was bawling, and I got pretty choked up too.

JESS: My mother-in-law fought for her marriage, and they are probably the most humble people I've ever met. As Christians, we fail. We're not perfect and never will be. But you don't have to be perfect and, anyway, it's impossible. That's why Jesus paid the price, and that's why none of us think we're any better than anybody else. Phil and Kay are my role models. Love and forgiveness are necessary for a marriage to survive. Forgiveness makes love possible.

Speaking of feelings, there's so much intense teasing between you and your brothers, Jep. Do feelings ever get hurt?

JEP: I love my brothers and would do anything for them. I know they feel the same about me. Alan has always been there for me with a nonjudgmental attitude, a listening ear, and wise advice. Jase is such a good teacher about wildlife, and he's the best speaker in our family. He studies, prepares, and he's always able to look at the funny side of life. I really respect his knowledge. I've always thought Willie is the coolest guy in the world. I've loved and looked up to him from the first moment I can remember. I'd tag along with him more than anybody else, and he took the time to teach me basketball and baseball. I copied him in just about everything, and I know sometimes it got on his nerves. I was so much younger than my brothers that I really didn't start stuff, but I sure didn't mind going to tell on them. They'd get spanked, and I wouldn't.

Jep, are you really Miss Kay's favorite?

JEP: Yes.

JESS: Miss Kay's favorite is whoever is with her at the time. The boys have tricked her before by asking her on speaker phone, "Mom, am I really your favorite?" She will always answer, no matter which son she's talking to, that yes, he really is her favorite. I do think she stood up a lot for Jep because his older brothers gave him so much grief. But they all like to tease, even Miss Kay.

What question do you get that really bugs you?

JEP: "How in the world did you get your wife?" I point to my beard and say, "There's dimples under here." I guess people are trying to be nice, and I take it as a compliment when they tell me my wife is beautiful.

JESS: Another question we get is, "Your show is fake, right?" That's easy. We are the same on television as we are in person. What you see is who we are and how we live our lives. Plus, look at Uncle Si. No one could make him up or write dialogue for him. That is exactly how he talks. But Si is the sweetest, kindest man I know, and I adore him. He loves to sit and tell stories to the kids. I've also had people tell me I'm prettier in person, or they remark on how little I am. That makes me think, *Am I ugly on TV? Do I look bigger on TV?* I've also had comments about how I married for money. Trust me. We wouldn't have had a trailer honeymoon if we'd had money when we got married.

Has being on *Duck Dynasty* made you more comfortable in the public eye?

JESS: I never thought I'd get up and speak in front of thousands of people. The show has made us braver. I'm willing to show the world who we are, to tell our story, and to use this opportunity God has given us to share His love and His Word with other people. Anyway, it's all from Him, and we know we are blessed.

JEP: I want to be a great role model, and so I'm willing to get up and tell my story, even the hard parts, if it will help others. I also want to help people get back to the old ways with hunting and how much joy it is to provide for your family. I don't ever want to lose that and be some kind of a rich guy who has it made. Also, I never want to move away from Louisiana. I want my kids to grow up with their grandparents, cousins, and uncles and aunts. I learned so much from my granny, and I want my kids to have those relationships and teachable moments too. There's something about being in a smaller town; the pace of life here is so different, but in a good way.

How would you feel about your kids going into show business?

JESS: There is potential for our kids to go on and do something in the entertainment industry, but we don't want to push them either way. We see how hard it is for some child stars to become famous at a young age and then go off the deep end when trying to transition to being less famous. We know you can't stay on top forever and want them to be well aware. We definitely want them to be mature in their faith; we want to prepare them for what's in the world but not be of the world. To always remember: faith and family come first.

Is there life after *Duck Dynasty*? What's next for you both?

JEP AND JESS: We're not sure, but it will most likely involve faith, family, and fashion.

About the Authors

JULES JEPTHA "JEP" ROBERTSON IS THE YOUNGEST SON OF PHIL and Kay Robertson. Jep grew up in the duck blind and utilizes these years of experience in his role as cameraman and editor for the family business. Jep is able to think like a hunter behind the camera and, therefore, captured excellent footage for the *Duckmen* DVD series. Previously, he also videoed footage for the *Benelli Presents Duck Commander* TV show.

Jep continues with the goal his father began years ago, to bring the "Duckmen style" of hunting out of the swamps, into the editing room, and into the homes of duck hunting enthusiasts around the world. Making his film debut in *Duckmen X* stoked Jep's passion for capturing his family's hunts on camera. That title remains his favorite Duckmen DVD to date. Jep and his family also star in A&E's hit series, *Duck Dynasty*.

JESSICA ROBERTSON AND JEP HAVE BEEN MARRIED FOR MORE THAN fourteen years. As Jep's wife, Jessica fits right in with the family. As a child she grew up hunting on the weekends with her father in the woods of Louisiana. She and Jep met in 2001, and they were married within two weeks of announcing their engagement. Jessica also has a business background, as do many in the Robertson family, but not from working at Duck Commander. She previously worked in real estate as a licensed real estate agent and most recently worked in sales.

JEP AND **JESSICA** LIVE IN WEST MONROE, LOUISIANA, WITH THEIR four children: Lily, Merritt, Priscilla, and River.

SUSY FLORY IS THE AUTHOR OR COAUTHOR OF EIGHT BOOKS, INCLUDing the *New York Times* bestseller *Thunder Dog*. She lives in California and is the director of the West Coast Christian Writers Conference.

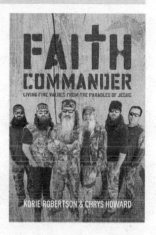